MOVING ON WITH
YOUR LIFE
AFTER A
DIVORCE

Key Takeaways, Analysis and Review
from a family law firm CEO

ALISTAIR VIGIER

Notion Press

Old No. 38, New No. 6
McNichols Road, Chetpet
Chennai - 600 031

First Published by Notion Press 2019
Copyright © Alistair Vigier 2019
All Rights Reserved.

ISBN 978-1-68466-242-5

DISCLAIMER

Dedication

This book is dedicated to all those going through difficult times.
Things will be better one day. Hang in there.

CONTENTS

PREFACE

During my time as a CEO of a law firm, I have met many clients who wish to obtain a divorce for a multitude of reasons. This can have profound effects on families. Therefore I decided to write a book to offer options using various case studies to illustrate how a new approach can change the outcomes.

INTRODUCTION

The question is simple: Are you really going to destroy your family, ruin the lives of your children, sell your properties and move into a separate apartment for a problem that counseling and a little personal effort might be able to solve? People don't understand the impact of divorce until they live through it.

The destruction is theoretical until it becomes a reality. They have a sense of its devastating effect on children, but they don't grasp the loneliness and alienation their kids will end up experiencing. Before the process begins, they don't understand how the divorce will change relationships with parents, siblings, and friends. Divorce can even lead to being fired because of distractions from work.

> *"Don't make a person you love constantly beg for forgiveness. Recognize that your partner has an inner goodness encouraging them to do the best he or she can. A loved one letting you down doesn't make them a bad person. It depends on how they own up to their mistake."*
>
> —*Alistair Vigier*

"Emily"

As with most mothers, Emily spent most of her time taking care of her daughter. Her daughter's name was Tricia, and when she went off to kindergarten, it felt to Emily as if she were entering a new phase in her life. The thought of returning to the job she had in marketing before getting pregnant scared her. Would she still fit in with these new age marketers? She barely knew what SEO was (search engine optimization.) Long gone were the days of yellow pages ads being the key way to get marketing results.

Emily had just turned forty years old, and she was in a transitional phase. She wasn't sure what she wanted out of life. She needed ways to combat the anxiety and depression she was starting to feel. It was starting to affect her psychically and mentally.

Emily decided to take up habits that would help her fight depression. She started practicing mindfulness, doing meditation, eating a healthy diet, and spending more time with her friends and family. She spoke to her family doctor, who decided to put her on Trazodone to help her sleep. She also went on Citalopram to help with her anxiety and depression. She started with a low dose to see if there were any side effects.

Emily spoke with her family about going through a divorce. They encouraged her to look at the transition in a different way. Instead of thinking that you are sleeping alone, think that you get the freedom to pick your own bedtime. You no longer must wake up in the middle of the night if your spouse coughs. They told Emily to look for little victories throughout the day.

Upon learning that Emily wanted a divorce, Steven worked to keep her, but when Emily refused his attempts at reconciliation— owing to a refusal on his end to acknowledge his narcissism— he became angry. They had accumulated assets of over 10 million dollars. They had a 6 million dollar home in the wealthy Toronto area of York Mills.

Steven made it clear that he would never settle despite her small demands. All she wanted was spousal support, child support, shared custody of Tricia, and to split the family-owned assets in half.

He was willing to take it to trial and draw it out as long as possible. He believed that because she was leaving him, she deserved to be punished.

Steven did not agree to any of her demands, which is rare in family law. As the couple spent 30,000+ dollars each on legal bills, Emily never ditched her positive approach or attempted to match her husband's aggression.

Steven tried to keep her from detaching in as painless a manner as possible. Emily withdrew from the relationship, free of emotional trauma, bitterness, or heartbreak. She also left with a thirst to begin a better life, accompanied by a deeper understanding of the type of partner that would support her.

Emily had to Google 'Toronto Family Law Firm' to find a family lawyer she could trust. She came across a family law firm called ClearWay Law and decided to book a consultation. She told the lawyer during the consultation that she didn't want to fight, she wanted to settle.

Emily was fine with either arrangement but hoped that it would not go to court. If the issue did not go to court, both Emily and Steven could have had a separation agreement done for $2000.

Emily's goals for personal growth is more important than watching her ex-spouse suffer. This has made her skilled at examining her own mistakes and recognizing what aspects of her life she has the power to control and change. She could have easily placed most of the blame for the marriage's breakdown at the feet of her narcissistic husband. Instead, she willfully took ownership of her situation.

Emily accepted partial responsibility for the failure of the marriage. As such, she did not feel like a victim. This allowed her to enter the divorce negotiations without feeling angry at Steven. Owning the mistakes she made her feel right, and she was very excited to enter a new relationship with a man better suited for her.

Emily now leads a happy life. Knowing what she will not tolerate in other people, she finds herself in a much healthier relationship with a loving man who doesn't care for yoga but loves that his partner does. The children are also adjusting well to the new family situation thanks to the great resiliency demonstrated by the mother.

Unfortunately, the former husband has persisted in his self-centered ways and chooses to have limited involvement with the children. Ideally, it's preferable for the parents to figure out a way to become friends and limit the amount of distress and disorder in the children's lives. But if one partner is not aiming for this dynamic, then the other person must work to free him or herself from the situation and not be held hostage by the whims and hateful emotions of the other person.

This book will help those going through a family law crisis. What I hope you realize from this book is that family law is very complicated, and it is better to get a lawyer to help you. I have built a client focused family law firm called ClearWay Law, and we would love to talk to you about your family law issue. Even if you don't live in Canada, you can still visit our website (www.clearwaylaw.com) and reach out to us. We will see if we can find you the right lawyer.

Our law firm also provides legal coaching to those who are self-represented (don't have a lawyer.) We can help answer questions about family law when you need us. I strongly believe that self-represented coaching is the future of family law.

For many clients, the breakup of the marriage feels like the end of the world. They believe the failure of the marriage somehow renders them a failure. Instead of embracing divorce as an opportunity to move away from an unhappy situation in hopes of establishing a better life, they allow anger, bitterness, and grief to set the tone for what will surely become a costly, drawn-out divorce.

"Lisa"

Lisa had an aggressive and somewhat controlling personality. At some point, her husband grew tired of these qualities, checked out of the relationship and demanded a divorce.

He was not narcissistic or abusive. Rather, he believed they were two people who were no longer compatible. Lisa felt like a failure as is common when a spouse asks for a divorce. The rejection, which she internalized, made her view her ex-husband as an evil person.

Lisa booked a consultation with our family law firm in Toronto. In the ClearWay Law firm overlooking Bay Street in Toronto, the family lawyer took a tough love approach with Lisa. The lawyer hoped she could become more self-aware and gain a wider perspective. She had to stop reducing the event into an issue of rejection. If she continued through life seeing herself as the victim, the attitude would permeate into all other aspects of her life. Around this time, she was passed over for a promotion at work which enforced her feeling of being the victim.

As the CEO of a law firm, I get to see the legal industry from a unique perspective. I find it amazing that some clients are willing to hire a family lawyer to represent them in their most important crisis (losing their house and/or kids) but sometimes don't trust their lawyer to invoice them for the actual hours worked.

I have heard countless stories where a lawyer sends a $40,000 bill for the work done that month to the client. The client freaks out and doesn't pay or can't pay. The law firm is left paying tax on the accounts receivable.

The best family lawyers encourage their clients to settle. The risk of losing your case and being left with a large legal bill (and having to pay the other sides costs) is very scary. The sooner the parties become more appreciative of each other's perspectives and take the time to 'walk a mile in the other party's shoes', the sooner they can settle.

A three-day trial in a family law court can cost you around $60,000.

It is the family lawyer's job to represent the client, not the managing partner of the law firm who wants to increase the lawyer's number of receivables at the law firm. Not all lawyers are simply interested in billing more hours. Many think they are offering support and showing understanding by allowing a client to vent about how they are the victim of their spouse. The family lawyer needs to take control of the conversation and explore the other spouse's position.

People will never settle if you do not accept partial responsibility.

It is very common for one or both parties to play the victim in divorce. The party that stayed at home cooking and cleaning feels that the other spouse never would have been successful in business if they had to take care of the home.

The 'breadwinner' says that they would have hired a housemaid and that all the other spouse did was go shopping. Everything the family has is because of the income that this spouse earned.

Shifting a client's perspective is difficult when there is this much hostility. Instead of seeing the divorce as a positive development, a chance to break away from a negative past, clients get stuck in their way of thinking.

Many clients think that they will never recover from divorce. In their minds, they have already lost their children, house, and friends. Instead, they should be coached by their family lawyer to see it as a stepping stone towards their next positive relationship. Most clients come out of a divorce much happier than before!

If you have a child, don't you want your children to see the best version of you? One that is free of pain and negative thoughts and actions? Don't you want to set a great example for your child about owning responsibility? Our family law firm has seen multiple situations where the ex-spouses get along much better than before the divorce.

This issue of playing the victim is not isolated to clients. Before starting ClearWay Law, I worked as a vice president for another family law firm. The managing partner had a very fragile ego. Only people that would feed his ego or 'lent' him money would be allowed to stay. As such, the firm had a massive turnover. Whenever a lawyer would leave the firm, the managing partner would say one of the following issues was the cause:

1. The lawyer was an alcoholic.
2. The lawyer had mental health problems.
3. The lawyer was having family problems.

The first few times I heard this, I believed him. After the 30th lawyer left the firm, I thought something might be wrong with the firm or the managing partner. I heard from my friends at the firm that when I left to start my own law firm, the managing partner had said it was because of mental health problems. A managing partner and a psychologist, he was multi-talented!

What was the managing partner doing? He was playing the victim.

He didn't want the staff to know that lawyers were leaving because of his poor treatment of them. He refused to believe that he had any faults. Even when the firm was near bankruptcy, and he had to borrow $200,000 from a staff member (which as of the writing of this book he never paid back), he still walked around the law firm with the ego of a god.

As the CEO of ClearWay Law, I decided my focus would be on treating our lawyers right. This keeps them happy and motivated. What do lawyers do when they are happy and motivated? They take great care of the clients!

What do happy clients do? They leave positive reviews on Facebook and Google and refer their clients to the law firm.

At the other family law firm I worked at, the cycle was negative instead. The managing partner treated the lawyers horribly. The lawyers were stressed and overwhelmed all the time. They were pressured to hit their target billings without the law firm spending money on marketing. The lawyers sometimes provided poor service to the clients, and the clients left poor reviews, complained to the law society, and told their friends that the law firm was terrible. The law firm was on a death spiral.

I knew there was a better way to do things. My law firm decided to try and offer a flat fee billing for all matters, even family law litigation. This is something that was extremely hard to do. We had to look back on all the clients that our family lawyers had represented and get averages on how much the legal fees were.

Flat fee billing clients builds trust between the client and the lawyer. The client no longer worries about getting overcharged as everything is clear up front.

Of course, some clients prefer hourly rates, and that's fine as well. We can offer either or. Some provinces in Canada allow for 'contingency fees' with the court's approval. Contingency fees are 'no win/no fee' which is very popular in personal injury and employment law.

We also have all our support staff work remotely. We have staff in Victoria, Vancouver, Regina, and Toronto, all supporting our Toronto family law firm. This enables us to keep our expenses down and to pass on some of the savings to our clients. When a client walks into a fancy office, they know it's paid for by the client's money.

I was recently featured in a major media company in Canada, speaking about remote working. You can find the story by searching 'Telecommuting on the rise to meet challenges of the real estate market, labor shortage' online. This appeared on CBC.

Many of us are searching for the meaning of life. We search because we believe the answers will provide our lives with balance, emotional wellness, and peacefulness. This level of balance is impossible if we are constantly concerned with how others view us and depend on people's Facebook 'likes' to boost our self-confidence. Our mood should not be correlated to the amount of notifications we receive.

Divorce is one of these instances. Examining your life through a wider lens will enable you to better understand the failure of your marriage, and the choices you made leading up to and during the marriage. With this newfound knowledge, you can begin planting the seeds for a more joyous and peaceful future centered not on making other people happy— family, spouse, friends— but on decisions aligned with your deepest convictions.

"If you're brave enough to say goodbye,
life will reward you with a new hello."

—*Paulo Coehlo*

Early in the process, you may not be receptive to the possibility of divorce being a growth opportunity. You're angry and hurting and want to hurt your spouse back. Generally, I believe that someone who begins the process with thoughts of wanting to inflict punishment on the spouse is crying out that he or she is in pain. What he or she wants is freedom from the pain.

At times, it can feel as if the world is pummeling you from all directions, and that you're powerless to stop the bleeding. In many ways, it's easier to relinquish control and not take responsibility for finding a way out of the mess. Through better choices, you can create a better future. You must rise above that lower sense of self that seeks chaos and revenge and tap into the divine spark we all possess.

Owning one's choices takes courage. We live in a world where most people fail to take responsibility, to admit they screwed up. Most people have trouble acknowledging they made a poor choice in picking a spouse. Whenever one of our lawyers brings up a client's role in the marriage's failure, he or she will answer, "He changed," or, "He pulled the wool over my eyes." The reality is that it takes two to create drama, and a situation where 100% of the blame falls on one spouse is extremely rare.

Approach divorce from the point of view that this is an opportunity to transition from a bad situation to something better. You will still be a family, but a different type of family. You will stop expecting other people to make you happy. Taking ownership of your situation, acknowledging partial responsibility for past behavior and mistakes doesn't make you a bad person. History's holiest and most noble people made mistakes, and some of the world's most consequential inventions, like penicillin, x-rays, and the pacemaker, were born out of mistakes.

Some of the greatest world leaders had tremendous personal failings, yet they were not bogged down by their unpleasant past and were able to make the right decisions at the right time. A healthy divorce means owning your past and forgiving the missteps of you and your spouse.

A healthy divorce is about understanding that you and your partner tried your best with the tools at your disposal. Maybe you each, in your own way, failed to deliver, but your motives at the outset were genuine and good. Your relationship was not conceived with one party setting out to destroy the other. You originally decided on the path of marriage to enhance your lives.

One spouse should not come out of a divorce on top. Both parties should feel as if they won and compromised on an equal level. They should feel as if they got to the best place possible and are ready to move on with their lives. This dynamic established at the end of the proceedings will set the tone for the future.

If one person feels like the winner, for example, then he or she will always have to feel like the winner when disagreements arise. Likewise, if a spouse feels like he or she lost, then every disagreement will be an opportunity to settle the score.

Letting past grievances, or even, triumphs dominate your thinking means your present considerations are taking the past into account at a time when you should be focused on the future. In life, you win some and lose some. Now, let it go and move on.

The opening credits of the 1970's sitcom *The Mary Tyler Moore Show* (a comedy about a single woman who moves to the big city after her boyfriend leaves her) perfectly illustrates the optimistic, positive outlook people should have when leaving a relationship.

The sequence opens with a throng of commuters pushing past Moore. She doesn't grimace or shield her face. Instead, she smiles, eager to take the lumps that come with the adventure of living on her own as a career woman in a major city. You can see her anticipation and excitement.

She believes amazing things will happen to her in this new life. The credits end with Moore, surrounded by a crowd of people in the street, twirling and tossing her beret high into the air. She's excited for the future.

This is the outcome you deserve at the end of your marriage. Where the outer layer, the anger, bitterness, and all the other emotions that have been weighing you down for years, is cast aside, enabling you to start fresh and head into your new life feeling excited.

CHAPTER 1

CAN YOUR MARRIAGE BE SAVED?

Within minutes of a client walking into our law firm for the first time, our lawyers can tell from a brief description of the marriage's problems whether reconciliation is a possibility. Not because they can see the future. Rather, from the few words exchanged they can get a handle on how the client thinks and whether he or she has the tools and mindset to work towards a solution.

"Jane"

Almost immediately after discovering her husband was having an affair, Jane stormed into our law firm. Divorce, in her mind, was the only option. Through our talking, however, it soon became clear to our lawyers that she and her husband had a solid, loving marriage despite the infidelity, which was a symptom of a specific, fixable problem.

The couple's only child is a severely handicapped son, whose day-to-day care left Jane and her husband, Mike, physically, emotionally, and financially drained. Over the years, this exhaustion caused them to lose touch with one another; life had ceased to be fun. After putting the child to bed, each spouse would shut down for the night.

This couple was not taking the time required to nurture the relationship. This one issue was ripping them apart. After Jane's anger over the infidelity abated, she began seeing the issue from her husband's perspective. She saw that her husband's cheating was not a rejection of her. He still loved her.

In fact, he loved her deeply. He was missing her and the feeling of closeness they once shared. I encouraged them to work on the marriage. By way of counseling, they succeeded at recalibrating the balance in their lives by cultivating a system of care for the child that would bring them closer together instead of tearing them apart.

They now have a healthier relationship, and the child's care feels less like a burden. No longer a source of tension, it has turned into something they do together with joy and love.

"...to have and to hold...for richer, for poorer," so goes the traditional wedding vow. Upholding the commitment through the 'richer' times of the marriage, the nice aspects of life together, like children and a comfortable home, is easy. But when two people are struck by 'poorer' elements— employment difficulties, a difficult in-law, infidelity, a severely handicapped child— they often allow it to overpower the 'richer' components and use it as an excuse to bail.

Many times the 'poorer' component of the marriage is superficial, like a personality flaw, but it takes on a power of its own. A spouse quickly loses perspective and begins believing this one issue sours the entire union. Here, an outsider— friend, lawyer, or counselor— can persuade a spouse or the couple that taking the 'poorer' along with the 'richer' is generally a worthwhile trade-off.

Too often people look to divorce as the immediate, best solution without ever stopping to ask whether the marriage is salvageable. In British Columbia, Canada, a wise statute requires lawyers to raise the possibility of reconciliation with clients and refer them to resources that can assist in charting a path to save the marriage. This law understands that an outside perspective, whether a counselor, therapist, or an insightful confidant, can mean the difference in a marriage's failure or success.

Caught in the middle of the chaos— anger, accusations, disappointments— is like being stuck in the fog of war. Or to throw in another apt aphorism, "You can't see the forest for the trees."

Even in cases where the other spouse may have committed a major transgression, as we saw in the case of Jane and her husband, providing context to a spouse's sins doesn't excuse the behavior. But it does help set a course towards forgiveness while providing release from patterns of behavior that may have taken over the marriage.

The anger may feel insurmountable. After all, it's easy to stay angry and, sometimes, it's hard to locate that love buried under the anger. But if you can succeed in moving past those feelings of enmity, and if you can alter your perspective, so you're no longer just the victim, then you can become a person whose marriage and the future isn't dictated by the actions of one person.

Your spouse isn't going to change unless you demand change and show a willingness to patiently support the transformation. If you make it, you will now be ready to take on any additional challenges life or your marriage throw your way, giving weight to the saying, "What doesn't kill you will only make you stronger."

In some situations, counseling or an outsider's perspective don't work. But most lawyers never even open their minds to the possibility of fixing the marriage. A client steps through the door, and the lawyer only sees dollar signs.

THE HISTORY OF DIVORCE

Once upon a time, marriage was cherished as an institution worth fighting to protect and save. Before the twentieth century, divorce was simply not an option in the Western world, thanks in large part to the culture and religion. In Judaism, for example, only a husband could grant a divorce, leaving the woman powerless. In the Catholic Church, only the Pope could annul a marriage.

Proving the radicalness and near impossibility of obtaining a divorce, we have the case of Henry the Eighth separating the

Church of England from the Roman Catholic Church to divorce Catherine of Aragon.

This conception of divorce remained unchanged until the turn of the twentieth century. It finally became recognized as an option in cases of adultery, although one would have to prove the adultery and name the parties involved.

Most people shied avoided such an embarrassing and messy legal situation, meaning divorce remained a rarity. Eventually, the definition of legitimate causes for divorce expanded to include cases of physical or mental cruelty. It still wasn't as simple as making a claim. Accusations had to be proven in a court of law and pass a high threshold.

The next shift in divorce occurred when courts began granting divorces based on separation or abandonment. This would spare litigants from having to prove ugly allegations like adultery or cruelty. In Canada, for example, a person could sue for divorce only after three years of separation.

After the three years, the courts would issue a decree nisi, which would stay the final order of the divorce until a period of ninety days had passed. This was a waiting period intended to give parties time to change their minds. Even in these moments of historical progress, we note stigma around divorce.

Decree nisi- An order will become binding later unless some condition is met

In the past several decades, attitudes towards divorce has swiftly shifted. Today, couples in Canada can divorce based on a one-year separation with a waiting period of thirty-one days. Most divorce cases are prosecuted on grounds of separation, meaning the parties are not forced to litigate based on allegations. Some jurisdictions even allow an instant divorce if both parties agree.

Historically, a divorce has never been easier to obtain.

There is, of course, a downside to this progress. The divorce rate in Canada and the United States is near fifty percent. In some Western European countries, the number is even higher. Belgium, for example, has a divorce rate of 71 percent. Spain, Portugal, and the Czech Republic all have rates over 65 percent.1 If laws merely reflect the will of the people, then we can interpret this progress as society's rapidly changing understanding of marriage.

Marriage is seen, more and more, as something temporary and impermanent. People no longer have the expectation that they will stay with the same partner for fifty years. They are getting married later, and many couples test compatibility before tying the knot by forming common law relationships.

DIVORCE ISN'T ALWAYS THE ANSWER

The disposable society we now live in is partially responsible for the high number of divorces. Every action is preceded by a thought, and thoughts today are influenced by cultures of reality television and celebrity that value short-term happiness and the right to act selfishly.

Taking lessons from reality television has no place in the decision of ending a family. Divorce requires slow, thoughtful deliberation. Gain control of your thinking and guard what you allow to enter your mind— the television you watch, the internet you surf, the friends you keep—. This is crucial. Only an outlook constructed on the understanding that your life is meaningful and impactful on those around you provides the perspective needed to weigh the 'poorer' against the 'richer', and to judge whether divorce is truly the least bad option.

A quarter of all divorces, in my view, are unnecessary. People think that other people can make them happy. It's not true. Only you can decide to be happy.

So, if they are unhappy, find themselves down in the dumps, they blame it on their spouses. Ultimately, what these people are saying is that love is conditional; if he or she doesn't provide something, then he or she is not a suitable spouse.

This is not surprising given we live in a culture of conditional love. Look at how parents or teachers withhold love from a child if he or she doesn't behave in a certain way. These parents set conditions for the relationship to manipulate the child's behavior. These same children grow into adults who display similar behavior patterns. In relationships, they withhold love from a partner if they don't receive what makes them happy.

Love, however, is not conditional. Love is about accepting the other person for who he or she is, not for what they can provide you. **Love should be continuous, not an emotion to be halted periodically when the other person does something you don't like.**

This doesn't mean you cannot point out bothersome behavior, but you should do so in a way that attacks the other person. Otherwise, you fill the person with guilt, which is the opposite of how you want a loved one to feel. You want someone you love to feel worthy of that love, not that they are a disappointment or insufficient.

Remember that people spend time on the things they love, and that makes them feel good. If you see your spouse as being something that hurts you, you will start to avoid them.

It doesn't make you a good person, either. Most people are doing the best they can with the tools at their disposal. Stop being judgmental. Stop being self-righteous. We adopt self-righteous attitudes to feel superior to other people, but how would the picture look if the mirror were turned on us. Would we be judged a perfect human being or a faultless spouse?

The grass is not always greener on the other side of the marriage as many people contemplating divorce like to imagine. It's possible to exit a marriage and begin a possibly better second stage to your life with a new partner. The chances that this will happen aren't good until you resolve any personal issues disturbing your current relationship. The color of the grass is tied to your internal state. If you don't change, you will just bring the issues from your current relationship to the next one.

Is your marriage failing because you have a poor relationship with money? You will bring that same attitude towards finances into your new relationship. Did your husband commit adultery, and you didn't stop to understand how you went wrong choosing this man? Don't be surprised if you find yourself in a similar position down the road. Also be aware that you might be attracted to 'bad boys' that may give you excitement.

Marrying an international sales manager versus an accountant that works a 9-5 will offer you different highs and lows. With the sales manager, your largest risk may be your husband cheating on you overseas. With the accountant, your biggest risk may be boredom.

You must bring 'you' into the next stage of your life. The threat of divorce is the perfect moment to try tackling any underlying personal issues, and it's a win-win strategy. If you do the work and succeed in fixing the area of concern, you may save your marriage. If the relationship is unsalvageable, you have bettered yourself and are now primed to enter a new situation without the risk of repeating your heartbreaking history.

PEOPLE CHANGE... AND THAT'S OKAY

Some marriages are in distress because the participants cannot accept that healthy marriages are meant to evolve over time. Marriages evolve because people evolve. A man's life values at age twenty may look different at age forty. A woman's craving for spirituality may intensify after having children. It may lessen. **Change is understandable and healthy, yet it's difficult for people to accept in a spouse, friends, or family.**

The person you marry at age 30 will change by the time they are 50 years old. How much have you changed in the last 20 years? Is your life different now than it was before?

It's rare to find a relationship where both parties welcome change and all the hurdles and bumps it may bring to the relationship. Most people avoid change at all costs. They are even willing to accept pain and sadness because it's a pain and sadness they know and can predict.

Maybe your spouse was big into fitness when you married them, and now they just come home from work and sit in front of the TV and eat.

> *"You know why divorces are so expensive?*
> *They're worth it."*
>
> —*Willie Nelson*

Change causes fear in people because the outcome is unknown. Spouses may go as far as trying to exert control over the other spouse to prevent him or her from changing. "This is not what I signed up for," he or she may claim. Or, a spouse may try to change the other spouse so he or she can have a partner for the journey he or she wants to experience.

Jane Fonda's marriage to Ted Turner survived numerous affairs early in the marriage thanks, in large part, to counseling. What ultimately ended up breaking them up was Fonda's spiritual change and her decision to keep her conversion to Christianity a secret from her husband.

As she wrote in her memoir, "I hadn't told Ted beforehand because by then I didn't feel we were on the same team… Alongside the frantic life we shared, I was living a parallel inner life, where I took care of my own needs. I also knew that if I had discussed my need for spirituality with him, he would have either asked me to choose between him and it or bullied me out of it."[2]

At age seventy, this woman was still growing and searching for how to become a better person, and her husband was not interested in taking part in her journey. They were moving into two completely different directions, and this was unacceptable to one of the parties.

Most relationships are based on the idea of two people feeding each other's egos. The expectation in all relationships is that the partner will make the other person feel as if he or she is a person of worth. This need is not met if a person's genuine attempt to change is met with ridicule and resentment, or if a person is made to feel that a change is in order.

It can be something small like changing the way he or she drives, manages money, talks at the dinner table, dresses, or thinks. Usually, the intention of the critical spouse is to have the spouse mirror his or her behavior and attitude, which is a rather narcissistic perspective. It's also judgmental for a person to think he or she knows what is right for someone else as if there is only one right way.

A healthy relationship is two independent agents who can accept, appreciate, respect, and love the differences in the other person. A marriage will only succeed if a person has room to grow, whether he is trying to garner a higher purpose about life or get to a better place emotionally. This doesn't free the person doing the change of any responsibility. He or she must communicate effectively to his or her spouse the changes being pursued and demonstrate sympathy for any potential impact it will have on the union.

Dr. Oz, the doctor turned television personality, is someone whose life has gone through remarkable changes. He and his wife have stayed married for over thirty years. He describes the couple's resiliency as follows: "I sometimes say that in twenty-seven years of marriage, I've been married to three different women, and Lisa's been married to three different men: **the student, the surgeon, and the talk show host.**

People do change during a lifetime, and we should view this as a positive instead of panicking and backing away. We don't want to stay static, because it's dynamism and newness that keep attraction and a marriage strong."[3]

Marriages that survive are ones that can adapt to change and see changes as opportunities for a more fulfilling tomorrow. **Darwin's 'survival of the fittest' is as true today as it was at the beginning of time.** You can't remain static in life. You must keep moving, or they will find you one day rotting in your La-Z-Boy chair with a beer gut.

A lifelong commitment is not a simple ask. Figuring out how to manage the relationship over the long haul can lead to an amazing life. It gets lonely flying solo, and it's nice to have a partner for the journey. Some men in their 20s and 30s find out that being a player gets old and depressing. No one throws you a parade when you have sex with over 100 people. Your reward might be an STD.

Connecting to others is important for most people, so if you can learn to be more accepting, rather than adopting a fallback position of rejection until proven otherwise, you will have better relationships and a fuller, more joyous life.

THE MOST COMMON CAUSES FOR DIVORCE

MONEY

Money, or financial stresses, is a major cause for divorce today. Two people can have wildly different approaches to money. One person may be a shopaholic, and the other saves every dollar. The problems are aggravated when couples don't communicate healthily about money matters. They don't sit down together and look at a monthly budget or make a joint accounting of the money coming in versus the money going out. Instead, they walk around muttering at one another over excessive purchases or stinginess.

Money issues are made worse in our day and age by credit being so readily available. Couples who think they are on the same page can take on too much. They buy the dream car or house, slightly out of their range, believing that a higher-paying job is around the corner or a promotion. This becomes a habit and, soon, they are buying nicer clothes, eating at finer restaurants and taking more luxurious vacations even though their incomes have stayed the same.

Many people want to be rich. **But if they cannot be rich, the next best thing is to feel rich.**

Suddenly, the couple is burdened with debt, and the debt becomes a tremendous pressure on the marriage, like Atlas carrying the world on his shoulders. Although, instead of the couple carrying the load together, working in tandem to formulate an offloading strategy, they stand in place sniping at each other about expensive tastes and whether the other person contributes his or her fair share. Meanwhile, the weight is crushing them.

Sometimes the financial issue affecting a marriage is not debt, but rather surplus. A wealthy couple will maybe have two or three houses, several luxury cars, and housekeepers. It takes tremendous time and resources to maintain this type of lifestyle. This leaves no room for the relationship to evolve in a healthy manner.

Fortunately, money is a fixable issue. Start with better communication. Couples can work on a budget together and make joint choices about what is affordable and what is not. There are many types of arrangements a couple can work out to solve this issue. Wealthy couples, for example, may decide separate accounts is the solution to bridging any divide over how to best manage and spend the family's money.

Sometimes the wealthier spouse will give the other an allowance. This might seem offensive to the spouse receiving the allowance, so go about it carefully.

Counseling can also play a role. If one spouse is a compulsive shopper, he or she can seek the help of a professional to produce a healthier relationship with money. The couple may need a therapist because they end up arguing every time they sit down to work on these issues. Money plays a crucial role in your life, but that doesn't mean it needs to control it, and it certainly should not doom your marriage.

ADULTERY

Sex, or a sustained lack of intimacy, is another reason marriages end. At times, the lack of sex can lead to adultery. The question then becomes whether the infidelity is purely physical, or whether it features an emotional element. Identifying a case of adultery as purely physical doesn't mean the betrayed spouse should feel any less compromised. It should be acknowledged that it allows greater space to work from to ultimately achieve forgiveness.

Emotional cheating is often worst for women than physical cheating. Finding out your husband is in love with other women may be worst than finding out they slept with an escort.

People do make mistakes. They are not with their spouses every minute of the day. They go off to work where they spend most of their waking hours, and they form close bonds with colleagues of the opposite sex. Again, the intention here is not to excuse the behavior but to appreciate the complexity of life. Over the course of a lifetime these types of relationships and temptations are normal and to be expected.

If you're the victim of such a betrayal, the hurt you will have experienced is real and understandable. You need to get past the anger to a point where you're thinking clearly and can consider what is worth preserving. This is a more constructive response than reacting to the injury by immediately proclaiming an end to the union.

It's about keeping your mind open to the possibilities of growth. Maybe the marriage can be saved; maybe an even stronger future together can be forged. Sometimes reconciliation is impossible; the pain is too much for a spouse to bear.

One client's husband— her high school sweetheart and a professional athlete— slept with— in his estimate— over a hundred women during his playboy days. Obviously, the man showed little discretion, and the public humiliation was too much for the client to overcome.

The actor, Steve McQueen, best known for *The Great Escape*, *Papillon* and *The Thomas Crown Affair*, was selling encyclopedias when he met his first wife, Neile Adams. In the marriage's next decade, McQueen became one of the highest paid movie stars in the world and began a series of somewhat public affairs.

His wife accepted this as a feature of the relationship. They had children together and lived an exceptionally luxurious life. She appreciated the emotional challenges her husband faced from growing up in a broken, chaotic home and the temptations he confronted as a mega-celebrity.

> *"Instead of wiping your tears, wipe away the people that made you cry."*
>
> —*Alistair Vigier*

Eventually, Adams entered an extramarital relationship of her own. It was when she finally came clean to McQueen about her own infidelity that the marriage crumbled. He couldn't accept that the other man was a fellow movie star. He claimed an electrician or a plumber he could have tolerated. The marriage turned abusive and violent, and they soon divorced.[4]

UNMET EXPECTATIONS

With some clients, divorce is a matter of one spouse failing to live up to the other's expectations. People enter marriages with expectations regarding things like respect, happiness, how they will interact with one another, or who will provide material support.

Oftentimes, expectations are not met because spouses are unaware of what is expected of them. Sometimes it's because they haven't articulated it to themselves. They got married young and never thought about long-term goals like where they want to be in ten years, or whether they want children and a house in the suburbs.

They didn't consider the role religion may or may not play in their lives moving forward. They may not have discovered what they want sexually. Maybe each spouse has a sense but has not had a deeper conversion with the partner about these issues.

In place of these conversations, assumptions are made, and rarely are they every accurate. Couples tend to raise the issue of expectations only when the gulf between them is largely obvious, at which point is often too late to work towards an understanding.

FAMILY

Parents can be major contributors to a child's divorce. Blood is thicker than water, and if marital discord develops, loved ones are quick to take sides. By doing this, they legitimize and harden the child's perspective. This makes compromise and resolution even more difficult. In addition, they may end up treating the spouse differently, adding further stress to the relationship. Finding a parent or relative that will urge the family member to look at the conflict from the spouse's perspective is rare.

Fighting on behalf of a child is understandable, but it can reach an unhealthy intensity and is, ultimately, a great disservice to the child. These days, parents will call the school principal demanding to know why a child received a poor grade, or a boss looking for an explanation as to why the son or daughter was fired. Instead of teaching the child how to take responsibility for a bad situation, the parent ends up enabling and encouraging disagreeable behavior.

FINDING REASONS TO STAY TOGETHER

People still idealize marriage as a lifelong commitment, which is why they feel a sense of failure when it comes to an end. They wish they could save it, but by the time family lawyers are involved, the issues have been piling up.

Between 2–5% of couples, in our law firm's experience, will opt to halt divorce proceedings and reconcile, a number far too low considering divorce's potentially grave consequences. Once proceedings begin, the spouses become too fixated on blaming the other person. Every problem is seen through this narrow prism that blocks out any memory of the shared 'richer' times of the past.

The couples that manage to stay together do so for a variety of reasons. Money can keep two people together. Perhaps the spouses have led separate lives for years, **but the wife is content and doesn't want risk forgoing her lavish lifestyle.** They may even see other people if they desire but stay a family so that the children will have stability. It's not ideal, but divorce isn't either. Not having enough money can keep a couple together, as well. The couple may need two incomes to pay off the mortgage and cannot even consider paying for a second residence.

Religious reasons might keep a couple together. Some faiths straight out forbid divorce, or, at the very least, make it difficult for a woman to obtain one, placing all the power in the hands of the husband. Maybe divorce is permissible, but family plays a central role in the religion's communal life, and a broken home is looked upon unfavorably and will make it harder for the children to marry later down the road.

Once a client from India told me that in his home country it is more socially acceptable to kill your wife than divorce her. I laughed assuming it was a joke, but his face showed he was serious. I am happy his wife lived in Canada.

In addition to money, religion, and, of course, children, couples find other motivations to reconcile. The 'team' may be too valuable or powerful to break up. Maybe they own a business together that is predicated on the marriage. Think of famous politicians whose infidelities have become public and how they managed to stay married. We cannot see into the hearts of the spouses, and we don't know for sure why they chose to stay. We must consider the possibility that they are putting personal ambition before love and trust.

These aren't extraordinarily positive reasons to stay in a relationship, but who are we to judge what works for people or question the trade-offs others make in life. There are couples who face exceptional trials but choose to work on overcoming the challenge because at the core of the relationship is a rewarding partnership based on mutual understanding and acceptance. They *can* appreciate how the 'rich' outweighs the 'poor'.

THE KEYS TO SAVING YOUR MARRIAGE

COMMUNICATION

Better communication is the remedy to many of the tensions and obstacles that test relationships. Whether it's a lack of intimacy, adultery, financial issues, change in a spouse, or the feeling that a partner is not meeting expectations, over the years, many couples fall into a pattern of not talking to each other in a meaningful, authentic, and vulnerable way. If you're inauthentic to your spouse, the one person who should not judge you, then chances are you're leading an inauthentic life.

Where communication is lacking, assumptions are made, and annoyances fester. People are quick to assume they are communicating effectively with a spouse. The lines have become so frayed over the years that the other person cannot hear what is being said or is in the habit of hearing what he or she wants to hear. Anticipating a spouse's negative reaction to certain conversations is enough to keep people from communicating certain fears and irritations.

COUNSELING

Helping professionals are widely available to make it easier for people to move in the direction of creating better marriages. A good family lawyer should have a list of counselors and marriage therapists to recommend. Counseling or therapy is worthwhile even if you cannot convince your spouse to join. Again, it can either help save the marriage or, at the very least, put you on better footing for the future.

Remember, many of these professionals chose their professions because they want to help. If you don't click with the first professional you see, find a different one. There are many resources online, as well, and useful books about all the problematic areas mentioned earlier in this chapter.

If you reach out to me on my law firm bio, I should be able to put you in touch with a counselor, therapist, psychologist, or psychiatrist.

FORGIVENESS

Forgiveness is key to saving any marriage. Forgiveness begins with appreciating your spouse. Anyone considering divorce is surely fixated on the bad or 'poorer' aspects of the other person. Employ the same energy to focus on the good, 'richer' aspects of the partner and relationship.

Start by thinking of the things you're grateful for in your life. You can be thankful for waking up in the morning, or the beautiful sunrise, or your first cup of early morning coffee. It's about putting yourself in a mindset that looks for the good in life. If you achieve this outlook, it will be easier to reach a forgiving place. All the bumps in the road appear as small cracks.

Forgiveness doesn't mean you have to accept everything your spouse throws your way. You may reach a point where you can no longer tolerate living with the sins and failings of the other person. Holding onto a grudge will prevent you from moving on with your life. The anger you hold onto is nothing more than the past playing over and over in your mind.

In his book *Necessary Endings*, Dr. Henry Cloud identifies three types of people: wise, foolish, and evil. One can sit down with a wise person and hold a constructive and critical conversation without the person reacting negatively. The wise person is open to feedback and will use it to improve them self. This person is not afraid of making mistakes and is constantly looking to move forward. Everyone should strive to be a wise person.

"I'm letting go. You let go a long time ago."

The foolish person possesses a fixed mindset. He or she doesn't see change as a possibility. When criticized, he or she will never take personal responsibility. It's usually somebody else's fault. This type of person is more concerned with reputation than actual performance.

The foolish person is not beyond hope. If they can become aware of the thinking patterns causing this harmful mindset and use the awareness to move away from an ego-driven existence to one that is growth oriented. If this is you or your spouse, it's well worth the effort to move him or her in the direction of becoming growth-minded so you can have a healthier and better relationship.

The evil person, on the other hand, is highly sensitive and takes offense easily. All the person's energy, emotional thinking, and thought patterns are directed at perceived injustices and trying to rectify them through retribution. Their biggest fear is others will be better off than them. They would rather die than say sorry.

You don't want this type of person in your life. Usually, there are deep-seated psychological scars to explain the behavior, and there is little you can do to influence change. The person will forever take offense and blame you for the smartest things. Before taking drastic action, you should speak with a psychologist to see whether you're dealing with this type of person.

In most cases, the question of whether a spouse's behavior can be reformed is essential when considering divorce. Consider the case of a serial adulterer. Some people claim it's a form of addiction. We hear the word 'addict' and our minds immediately go to drugs and alcohol. They get used to cheating on their spouse, and it becomes a habit. The habit over time becomes an addiction that is hard to break.

There are many other types of addiction— food, adrenaline, sex. Unmet obligations, financial difficulties, and strained relationships are indicators of addiction.

Our culture and way of life has made it easier to be swayed into bad, addictive behavior. In recent years, I've witnessed how pornography and online gambling can destroy people. Both activities can remain harmless, but the internet making them readily available increases the odds that somebody will turn obsessive. Soon, the husband is not showing interest in sex. Maybe he is dipping into the family's savings account so he can play another online gambling game.

A client of our law firm was suffering from sex addiction. He was a successful sales manager who sold millions of dollars of products per year. He saw chasing women as the same thing as selling products. It was all about the chase. Once the goal was achieved, it lost its value. It was time to move on the next 'goal'.

He did not drink, smoke, gamble, or use drugs. He lived a perfect life from the outside. To deal with his anxiety, he would use Tinder after a 12-hour shift at work. He would spend his nights going on walks with women. To keep up his energy for work, he would look at porn in the morning and at night (if a woman wasn't over that night.) Sometimes he would cancel his dates so that he could have a break from sex. Instead, he would look at fetish porn.

He enjoyed the playboy lifestyle at first. He soon realized that he couldn't sit for thirty seconds without his mind raising. After a year of living that lifestyle, it got tiring. He was tired of having people come in and out of his life. He wanted to start a relationship.

He tried to quit sleeping with others but struggled. Messaging women online had become automatic. He started relationships with women, but they would find out about each other, and it would fall apart. Eventually, he had to decide whether to only sleep with one woman or live the playboy lifestyle forever. I am happy to announce he is now in a committed relationship.

Some addictions are worse than others. Someone addicted to hard drugs runs the risk of dying. A gym rat's body may be healthy, but his deep commitment can still cause chaos in his life. Can't curb your behavior after witnessing a negative situation? It's a possible sign of a deep emotional instability that needs fixing.

Witnessing such behavior in your partner doesn't mean you should immediately give up on them. There are ways of treating and fixing these addictive behaviors. There may be different rates of success depending on the type of addiction. In all instances, an open line of communication between spouses is crucial. This is an opportunity to demonstrate support and a willingness to work through the issues as a unit. The spouses should agree on a plan for addressing the problem.

If he or she has made a sincere attempt to fix the problem and is still stuck in this pattern of behavior, then, maybe, it's time to bail. Ultimately, it's your choice as to how long you will stick it out. Through 'richer and poorer' should mean, at the very least, that you don't open from the position or viewpoint that the marriage or your spouse are unsalvageable.

This is the person your married. You would want your spouse to cut you some slack and provide room to maneuver if the roles were ever reversed. We are all human. We all make mistakes. We all deserve, at the very least, an opportunity to change from our loved ones.

Divorce, however, is the only option in virtually all cases of physical abuse. Changing the behavior of an abuser is too difficult and risky. It takes a genuine commitment to change. Too often people are prepared to stay in a marriage if the spouse merely voices an interest in getting help. That's not enough. The abused should run for the hills. Consider coming back only if the abuser has taken legitimate steps towards dealing with his or her inner problems. The odds of this happening, we must remember, are low. We are talking years of therapy. How many black eyes will you receive in these years of waiting?

If you cannot leave a violent relationship, you need to reflect on why this person, who is causing such pain, has an emotional hold on you. Why are you willing to tolerate it? You must examine the nature of your relationship. You may depend on your spouse for money. Maybe being with the person fulfills some deeper emotional need.

The larger question to ask is where is your self-worth? Is your opinion of yourself so low that you don't think you're worthy of better treatment? If you're staying for the children, you should consider what effect this will have on them. In matters of love and marriage, children look to their parents as the first point of reference.

Do you want them to see this dynamic as normal and acceptable? Do you want them immersed in a violent atmosphere? It's not worth walking around black and blue, or worst, ending up dead just so your child can have a father.

In the end, people have free will. If they want to divorce even for a rectifiable reason, it's the job of a divorce lawyer to help them understand they are responsible for the decision and help them let go of the relationship in as healthily a manner as possible.

QUESTIONS YOU SHOULD ASK BEFORE CONTEMPLATING DIVORCE

1. Why am I thinking about divorce?
2. Have I talked this through with a family lawyer?
3. Is my marriage the problem, or is a finite stress causing temporary tension (loss of a job, the death of a parent, a child's troubles)?
4. Is the problem merely a lack of time together, or lack of good health?
5. Is there a substance abuse problem that can be addressed before moving towards divorce?

CHAPTER 2

LETTING GO

Expect overpowering emotions to strike once you make the decision to divorce. Appreciate that these feelings can disturb the process as you move forward. Securing a healthy divorce requires completing an emotional separation from your spouse. This needs to happen before any documents are signed, and even before the terms are negotiated.

DIVORCE FEELS LIKE DEATH

The predominant emotion expressed by clients in my law firm at the beginning of the process is anger. They elaborate on the reasons for the marriage's collapse. Sometimes the anger is tinged with bitterness and grief. Handing grieving client's tissues or throwing a supportive arm around the back is not an uncommon scene. Allowing a client to vent for the first few meetings is usually enough to clear the raw emotions from the mind. This happens to both men and women.

"Ellen"

Now and then, however, I get a case like Ellen, where the client is utterly grief-stricken and faced with a sense of paralyzing loss. Ellen knew her marriage had its problems but accepted them as status quo and normal for any twenty-plus-year marriage, so her husband's call for a divorce left her shocked and depressed.

She could not get out of bed, go to work, or care for her children. It was as if the love of her life had died. (Feeling as though one cannot live without the other person is often a clear indication that one is involved in a codependent, unhealthy relationship destined to fail.) It was clear Ellen would not overcome her sense of loss until she arrived at a point where her happiness was not dependent on her husband. In short, she needed to find internal sources of happiness. In addition, to fully let go she had to understand that life would continue even if he were no longer a part of her life.

A lawyer must be particularly careful when dealing with someone in Ellen's state. Her thinking was cloudy, stuck in the past, and she was not in the right frame of mind to resolve anything or make good decisions about the future, how to divide the money, and childcare responsibilities. Some lawyers would feel comfortable advancing Lisa's case without pause, believing they can make the right decisions for the impaired client. These lawyers are carrying out a great disservice. In divorce, the means and process are equally, if not more, important as the ends in terms of gaining closure and letting go of the past.

Time is the preferable strategy for a client like Ellen. One of our lawyers slowed down the process by asking the husband and his legal team to provide us with space and time so that Ellen could seek professional help. In the interim, the two sides crafted agreements around money, custody and living arrangement to help guide the separated couple's lives over the next year. It took Ellen a little more than a year to work through the grief and overcome the shock of this sudden turn in her life. Finally, she saw that this was not the end of the world. Fortunately, we had a husband who was sensitive to her fragile state and was willing to stall the process. Eventually, the case was resolved in meditation. This was thanks to Ellen being in the right emotional state to negotiate objectively and make business-like decisions.

DEAL WITH THE EMOTIONS FIRST

You must accept you're divorced before you can go through with the divorce. You must lose any feeling of dependence on the other person. No longer looking to the other person for happiness or financial support should be freeing. You're being forced back to a natural state where you obligated to create your own happiness and good fortune. If you could have succeeded in making this transition during your marriage, then maybe it would have been saved. The most glorious relationships are those where both parties stand as independent people who are not constantly working to please the other person but gaining this freedom now will certainly help in future relationships.

Anger, as mentioned above, is the most common of the dangerous emotions coursing through the minds of clients at the initial stages of the divorce, and the most contested, expensive divorces are the ones where both spouses are equally angry. Anger, some contend, is a healthy emotion. Don't repress it. Get it all out. It's natural. This is true, up to a point, a limited point. Anger becomes a problem when it's released as a reaction instead of a well-calculated response with an intended goal.

"No relationship is ever a waste of time. If it didn't bring you what you want, it taught you what you don't want."

The ideal client for my law firm is already in the process of emotionally letting go of the marriage. The client is not interested in allowing his or her anger to dictate the process. In a perfect scenario, both spouses have reached this point. Pausing the proceedings so both parties can get on the same healthy page is not always an option. Sometimes the other lawyer is not interested in delaying.

When this happens, it's up to the distressed client's lawyer and other professionals to help the client deal with the anger or grief as soon as possible. This allows the client to have a more harmonious divorce. If you think your marriage is coming to an end, the time is now to seek counseling, before the separation happens. A healthier mindset that is less focused on negative feelings towards your partner means a smoother, less costly divorce and the increased likelihood of creating a working post-divorce relationship with your spouse.

Divorce proceedings, too often, become a way for the still attached spouse to hang on. In some situations, spouses are in touch with the anger or grief. They believe only a generous settlement will free them of these emotions. Once they get the large settlement, however, they are even more heartbroken because now that the divorce is complete. They have now lost another link to the spouse. It never ends for these people. They are hanging on to the thinnest of threads, to constantly stay engaged with their exes. They will take any small disagreement right to their lawyers and will continue to spend money and waste time after the agreement is signed.

Allowing time for clients to work on themselves and any emotional issues before negotiations begin sounds reasonable. There are many lawyers that prefer their clients to feel victimized and angry. For these lawyers, a longer process, and a possible trial means more money. They get the clients so worked up. Who gets flight points? Who is responsible for taking the child to gymnastics? This turns into a mountain of litigation and increased fees.

Wanting to obsess over arguments, instead of moving on, makes sense. The unknown nature of the future is enough to strike panic in all of us. Letting go of anger and grief means coming to terms with the past. You need to free up your mind in order to think about future opportunities and possibilities with excitement instead of fear. People dealing with depression, for example, feel as if they'll never experience relief. No remedy seems to work. They may even wish they were dead. Then, finally, therapy does work. The pain vanishes and, months later, they can't even access those earlier feelings of desperation.

Everything in life is cyclical, from the weather to the stock market. The weather is sometimes sunny and sometimes rainy. Life is never the same day in and day out. There will be crummy days, great days and plenty of days in between. Try to remember there was good at one time in this relationship, and there will be good again in a different relationship. This awful thing happening to you at this point in life that is bringing you low is not a reflection of what your life is or where it's headed.

It stands out as being particularly painful because it's unique and not the norm. Remember, you're in the middle of getting out of a bad situation. You have taken to reading this book because you want to come out of the divorce stronger than before. The hard part is done. You're learning a great deal about yourself from this experience. You're ready to reencounter some good in life on the way back up.

WHY EMOTIONS RUN HIGH

"Katherine"

Emotions run especially high when one spouse's sense of self is tied to his or her partner. Katherine was married to a famous politician, who was a hero to some, a villain to others. He was constantly in the news, and the wife became quite captivated by the fame his job brought them. She enjoyed the rich and glamorous social life they now enjoyed. She had become a minor celebrity because of her husband even though he was the one who attended council meetings and met leaders from all over the country. The identification with her husband was so strong that, when among friends, Jane had the habit of answering questions for her husband. She mistook his life for hers. She never took the time to carve out a life or identity of her own. When the marriage collapsed, it felt to her like a part of her body was being cut out. She had no sense of what she would do with her life. She had no idea how she would spend her days.

Usually, the codependency is on a smaller scale, the spouse being someone who provides him or her with joy, money or stability. When the person goes away, the other spouse is left asking, "Who am I without this person?" If you have trouble answering this question, you will have difficulty moving forward even after the divorce.

Anger, bitterness, and grief can also be consequences of shock. A spouse may know that the marriage is not the greatest in the world. He or she has come to accept the status quo and believes the other spouse holds similar feelings. The spark is gone, but they eat breakfast in the morning together and watch television at night. So when they hear their partner wants a divorce, it shocks them. Often, it's a case of one spouse turning a blind eye to changes in the partner. There is a reason many couples divorce at the age when midlife crises hit. (Personally, I prefer the word 'challenge' to 'crisis'.)

As a man nears his fifties, his children and the youthfulness they represent begin to leave the house for the grownup world. Questions of mortality begin to loom large. Fighting to hang onto his sense of youth, the husband maybe takes up motorcycle riding. The wife thinks of the husband's new hobby as nothing but a childish pursuit. Or the roles are reversed, and it's the wife who begins taking better care of her body. She joins a running club, while her husband continues his sedentary life in front of the television. Soon, she is hanging out with other women runners, and they go out together on Friday nights. Casual dinners slowly turn into her coming home drunk in the wee hours of the morning.

Both these scenarios can lead to situations where the spouses make new acquaintances, possibly even entering extramarital relationships with people to make them feel younger and more alive. These aren't uncommon scenarios. It only takes one person in the relationship to feel the need to fill an emotional void. Soon there are talks of divorce.

FIXED VS. GROWTH MINDSETS

We have outlined the many situations where a spouse might react to the divorce with anger, bitterness or grief. If these emotions are not extinguished early, they can quickly turn to feelings of victimization. This is when divorces can turn ugly because a victim mentality implies the belief that the person has no power in this world. He or she is purely an object.

The victim believes he or she has a limited existence. Either a situation is forced on the victim, or the victim is forced into a situation. This person has what the psychologist Carol Dweck refers to as a fixed mindset.

In her book *Mindset: The New Psychology of Success*, Dweck identifies two disparate outlooks. The fixed mindset belongs to someone who grew up constantly being told of his or her specialness. The person, therefore, sees his or her qualities as fixed and unalterable.

After all, why would you want to tinker with perfection? Every situation, therefore, needs to verify this specialness. There is no room to negotiate because sharing space with the other threatens to damage the idea of his uniqueness.

A growth-minded individual, on the other hand, is a person who is continually developing and sees all obstacles as challenges to grow. For the growth-minded individual, a situation can always be changed, and failure is never an option. They can take the blame for a less than ideal situation and see it as an isolated misstep. In fact, they take pride in learning from their mistakes.[5]

In cases of divorce, people with growth mindsets take responsibility for their situations. This is not to say they don't think their partner contributed to the mess and are partly to blame. They know, however, that they cannot control what the other person will do or think. They can only control themselves.

The spouse with the fixed mindset and victim mentality will take a more combative approach to the divorce proceedings. They will spend their energy identifying instances where they have been slighted or wronged. Everything in their lives is seen through this narrow prism. They take comfort in playing the victim card and knowing that nothing is their fault. Fixed-minded people believe that admitting mistakes makes them out to be bad people. Staying in a relationship with this type of person is quite difficult. One can imagine the impossibility in trying to formulate an agreement based on everyone's true interests.

"Ellen"

Ellen came to my law firm grieving, a clear sign she possessed a fixed mindset. The divorce was something that hurt her. She could not imagine why she was no longer desired. In her mind, nothing would ever be right again until everything was put back into its original place. At that moment, all our lawyer's energy was invested in moving her in the direction of becoming a growth-minded person. The lawyer knew this would enable her to bring this divorce to a close with minimal pain. Further, she'd be able to begin contemplating a new life without her husband.

Professionally, the greatest reward is when a lawyer can have a transformational influence on a client's life, as opposed to one that is purely transactional. In my personal life, I am constantly striving towards self-improvement. I work towards goals in all areas of life, and I desperately want others to share this outlook.

Most lawyers start their law firm to center on money and status. When I created ClearWay Law, I wanted it to be a growth experience. I wanted to impact people in a positive manner. One of my great talents lies in shortening the distance between people, mainly through getting them to talk. I'm a peacekeeper at heart. As the oldest child, I felt it my responsibility to help keep the peace. I became a specialist in redirecting rage and moving it onto less delicate targets.

DO IT FOR THE KIDS

Working through feelings of anger and grief before and during the divorce process is particularly important if children are involved. The minute you decide to have a child, you must become more self-aware of the thoughts that enter your mind and the words that leave your mouth. Children notice and hear everything. Nobody is expecting you to be the perfect parent, and you should always be authentic with your children. You must be cognizant of the fact that your current actions will influence their future behavior. If you're constantly swearing at your spouse every time you get into an argument, the child will grow up thinking this is normal. They will see it as a healthy way to argue with a loved one.

Divorce is the perfect opportunity to model good behavior for the children. Explain that everyone makes mistakes, but what is important in life is to take responsibility for them. You can instill in the children a growth mindset that understands the benefits of mistakes. Show the children your willingness to take on challenges and risk. Teach them to never be so hard on themselves that they end up thinking they are bad people. Model the difference between reactive and responsive behavior. The responsibility of parenthood is awesome, and it doesn't allow for breaks. A child is on twenty-four-hour surveillance.

Some parents believe they can shield the children from the divorce. Even if you're not bringing them into the lawyer's office, they will notice your disposition after your return home and hear your blow-by-blow to your friends and family later that night. A child will see how a parent acted during the divorce and whether the father or mother held a fixed or growth mindset.

"Be with someone who brings out the best in you, not the stress in you."

Down the road, what happens if your child were to choose the wrong partner? Don't you want him or her to know that it's possible to go through a divorce in a harmonious fashion? Show them that parents can remain friends, respectful and loving of one another, even after a divorce. It will help them become people who are adaptable and don't treat every bump in the road like it's the end of the world.

Behaving in this evolved way isn't a good opportunity for only your children, but your family and friends, as well. Successfully modeling a growth mindset during a divorce strengthens the social fabric. It's two fewer people involved in chaos and drama. You and your spouse owe it to your children and the world to do a good job of this.

If the spouses are on good terms and are both growth-minded people, then a winning scenario is possible for everyone involved, including the children. Another key element of crafting a winning scenario is giving the children a true, authentic voice in the process. This means never dragging them into court. They would have to sit in front of a judge and choose between mommy and daddy. Child specialists are a safe, non-traumatic resource to get at the heart of what a child wants in terms of future arrangements. Many parents think they have open lines of communications with their child. But they are deaf to the reality that the child is usually telling the parent what he or she wants to hear.

There are professionals that can help you arrive at the right place emotionally, so you can begin building a better future for this new iteration of your family. Holding on to the relationship through feelings of anger and grief will cost you time and money, and you will never find relief for the negative emotions currently stalling your progress. If anything, they will intensify as you battle your spouse.

At times, the universe sends us messages either through the people in our lives or life-changing events like a death or divorce. Usually, it's a sense of hope, a challenge to see the best in ourselves, other people and the world, and to realize that how we feel today is not how we will feel a year from now. Change is forever coming. There will be opportunities to rejoice. Only through opening our hearts and minds to these messages can we begin to take accountability and let go of our past.

CHAPTER 3

SEEING YOUR DIVORCE AS THE BEGINNING OF A (GREAT!) NEW LIFE

Crafting a separation agreement is about negotiating a new future for you and your family. Most people dread this stage of the divorce. The reality sinks in, and they start envisioning a morose future of transporting children between two houses. They are also expecting arguments with the ex and bad dates. You should relish this opportunity to create a better life. First, feel thankful that you're leaving what you have determined is a miserable and hopeless situation. Second, have confidence that your life will improve assuming you're willing to learn from your mistakes.

HOW DIVORCE CAN BE A SPRINGBOARD FOR A BETTER LIFE

"Greg"

Greg has as much reason as anyone to hold negative attitudes towards marriage. He retained our law firm when his first marriage was ending. In his late twenties, he married a younger woman with a whole host of issues. Part of Greg's problem is that he is an overly generous person. Instead of heading for the hills soon after he became aware of her troubles at the relationship's outset, he determined to try and save this woman. They soon married and quickly had two children. Motherhood only intensified his wife's issues, and she began drinking heavily. Greg tried sticking it out, but the wife refused to commit to helping. Finally, for his and the children's sake, Greg decided to end the marriage.

Entering the proceedings, his main goal was to get custody of the children. The ensuing custody fight wasn't perpetrated out of spite. At all times, he had the children's welfare in mind. He knew that his wife was not in the right mental state to mother the children. In all other matters— alimony, housing, assets— he acted kindly and generously towards his spouse, even though the marriage's collapse could be blamed, mostly, on her difficulties. He took ownership of the situation, accepting that he had chosen to ignore any red flags and start a family with this woman.

His wife put up a fight, but he stuck to his position, refusing to compromise on the custody issue, yet searching for ways to bridge the divide in all the other areas. Deep down, the wife knew she was not fully capable of caring for the children. She possibly saw that the boys naturally gravitated towards the father. Eventually, the couple reached a settlement that made Greg a single dad to two boys.

The growth mindset Greg carried through the divorce proved indispensable as he raised the boys. Surely, the children saw in their father a man who didn't walk around playing the role of a victim looking to settle scores. Rather, they observed a man who was working to improve the family's situation through better choices. Soon after the divorce, Greg remarried. The marriage, unfortunately, lasted less than a year. Once more, our firm helped Greg with the divorce. Greg was looking to provide a mother figure for the boys. He enjoyed the company of a woman different from his first wife. He had rushed into the second marriage with this woman. With relative ease, we resolved the situation. Again, the absence of a victim mentality on Greg's end proved essential.

The third time was a charm for Greg. His current marriage has lasted more than a decade. He is in his fifties now, and his boys, who are grown men, have a wonderful relationship with their stepmother. Not coincidentally, Greg's restaurant, after a decade and a half of stagnation, blossomed, and he has grown exceedingly wealthy. His mind is no longer occupied with trying to save people or make them happy. He is free to focus on actualizing his plans and ambitions.

Fortunately, Greg came to our law firm with a growth mindset and an upbeat attitude. Allowing him to plow through the many difficulties life threw his way was an ability to ask the right questions. It also helps that he has an unwavering belief that he will come always come out on top. Not in relation to the ex-spouse, but in terms of life and the person he was before the adversity.

To our lawyers, there was never a need to shift him past a victim mentality. If someone starts the process as a growth-minded individual, as Greg did, they will likely not give up this outlook even if anger and bitterness are injected into the proceedings by the other side. This tells me that, once obtained, a growth mindset becomes an almost permanent feature of one's personality. If only all our clients were this easy. The ones, like Greg, who are innately positive thinkers, succeed in transitioning out of their troubling, loveless marriages into a successful future.

In our society, people tend to marry at a relatively young age. Over time the values and interests of the spouses change. It can reach a point where the spouses each feel bad about pursuing the lives they want to lead, so they repress feelings and wants, or go behind the partner's back. The secrecy and repression come because of having been conditioned to stick to the union no matter the circumstances.

At some point, though, it becomes wrong to hold onto something that is clearly not right. It's wrong to treat yourself that way, not to mention, your spouse and children, who can easily sense the unhappiness in a parent. Do you want your children thinking of life as a punishment? Or should they know that there is always the possibility of pursuing more beneficial and fulfilling options?

LET PROFESSIONALS HELP YOU MOVE BEYOND THE EMOTIONS

Most clients don't walk into my law firm with the mentality that life will get better because of the divorce. They don't see the conflict as a learning opportunity, a seed for a better future. If anything, they feel as if everything is going to hell in a handbasket. To change this outlook, however, there are certainly practical steps other lawyers and I can set in motion.

I start with a tough love approach. The love part of the equation is essential, because if the client feels as if his or her anger and other feelings aren't being regarded, they'll reject any plea to get past those emotions. They need the pain validated before they can move on. Some clients, after months and months of talking, cannot overcome their current mindset, which indicates they will carry this past misfortune into their future unless they get outside help.

In the end, lawyers are not trained psychologists, even if many gain a great deal of understanding of human behavior. In these situations, helpful professionals specializing in conflict resolution can help move a client away from his or her current thought patterns.

Even when the couple is not trying to save the marriage, a counselor or therapist can be useful in getting parties through the divorce. Not all mental health professionals are created equal, and you must find one who is the right fit. Trying to evolve from a fixed to a growth mindset? You should steer clear of a professional who is simply interested in reinforcing your victim mentality.

People do have the capacity to naturally work through the various emotional stages that strike at the beginning of a divorce. They can eventually reach a point of acceptance on their own. When dealing with divorce, time is of the essence. The quicker he or she will finish the bleak chapter that was their marriage and start a more promising one. This is true in all areas of life. Some people allow adversity to get them down for an entire year.

They fall into a deep depression, while others can get over the same type of misfortune in a day. Everyone is different.

A mental health profession and a good lawyer will impress upon you the idea that everything you're experiencing, someone before you has already experienced. This insight can help you move away from any sense you're some unique victim at the mercy of the world. Your thinking patterns will start shifting, and suddenly you will feel more emotionally stable and will find freedom from the fears and anxieties that have come to dominate your thinking.

I have a friend who has a fear of tsunamis. To get over the anxiety, she took pills, refusing to speak to a therapist about her phobia. At some point the pills no longer worked, so she copes by avoiding beach vacations. Think of the sacrifice she makes all because of her unwillingness to seek professional help. The thinking patterns you're looking to change coming out of a divorce are more impactful than not going on a beach vacation. They affect every aspect of your life. Also, by becoming more aware of your thinking, you begin to appreciate what you allow to enter your mind.

I don't watch the news. They earn revenue by selling stories that trick you into being angry or afraid with misleading headlines. As soon as I 'un-liked' all the news on Facebook, I found I was a happier and more relaxed person. I don't need to hear about a bomb that went off in Africa killing hundreds.

Financial anxieties prevent many people from embracing the future with excitement. They are unsure of how the divorce will impact a certain lifestyle they wish to maintain. Even in cases where there is no worry about money, financial issues may keep a spouse engaged in the divorce in an unhealthy way.

Some angry clients feel that the spouse is trying to shield money. One person might have overseen the finances during the marriage. The other one doesn't have a good accounting of all the monies. In such cases, adding a financial advisor to the team of advisors can help clients understand what things are worth in present and future terms. This helps paint a fuller picture so there are no lingering questions, distrust or doubt that might prevent unease or enmity.

In some ways, a marriage is like a business, making a divorce like a break up of two merged companies. A lawyer is not a CFO even if he or she has a good handle on money matters in marriages. It's important to have a financial planner to assess assets, provide financial advice and help disentangle the finances. This is another person who can help shine a light on the reality of your current and future situations.

The team you have assembled— lawyer, mental health professional, and financial advisor— should help you arrive at a mindset where you drop past concerns and begin to embrace the more glorious future around the corner. Additionally, there are plenty of books and internet resources providing encouragement and helpful advice regarding all the issues mentioned above. There is a list of helpful resources on the ClearWay Law website.

EMBRACE CHANGE

A person stepping into our law firm excited about what lies ahead post-divorce is an exception. Often, it's men who are eager to start that next phase of life, especially in a case where they have met a younger woman and are once again experiencing that youthful feeling of falling in love. This type of client will demonstrate his eagerness to move on by acting generously towards the wife, especially if financial resources are available to him. They may even act out of a sense of obligation. They feel that they should take care of the mother of their children.

Persuading a client who is younger to get excited about what lies ahead is easier since he or she can see how much life there is yet to live. That argument becomes more challenging to sell when dealing with someone who is over fifty and is already thinking about issues of mortality— even if people are living longer than ever. The goal for every client, no matter the age, is to get the client to think about the future in a more positive fashion.

People call me and want help getting divorced. I can get a sense of what is important to the client and use that information to the get the person excited about what is to come. Maybe the person felt held back in a certain area of his or her life. He wished he had traveled more. She wanted more children. Divorce allows the person to undo reverse all the regrets of missed opportunities. The other option, holding a pity party for the next two years, fighting with the spouse and spending over $100,000 on family lawyers sounds far less appealing.

Periods of crisis, like divorce, is where we see ourselves in a completely different fashion. These are the moments where we can ask what went so terribly wrong, making them great catalysts for change. Not unlike a drug addict who enters rehab after surviving an overdose, the end of a marriage is a rock bottom that can trigger deep introspection. Here is a coupling that began with joy and promise and has devolved into bitterness and misery.

This is the seed for change, the universe making you come face-to-face with your downward turn and forcing you to ask the tough questions. What has led to this moment, and what can you do to reverse the momentum? If not now, when? If not you, who? What elements of this situation do you own as your responsibility? What factors contributed to you choosing the wrong spouse? What role did you play in the marriage's collapse?

If you decide to condemn someone else for ending up in this crisis, then understand that any time you face adversity in life, you will end up blaming someone else. If you go looking for alibis for your own failures, you will find them. None of us want to leave the planet thinking we didn't live the best life we could have lived.

> "Accept what is, let go of what was, and have
> faith in what will be."
>
> —Sonia Ricotti

In my career, I've seen many clients who embrace this chance for a second shot and end up gaining total control over their lives. They accomplish a complete metamorphosis, and they emerge from the divorce like a caterpillar that has turned into a beautiful butterfly.

Sometimes the fixed mindset client becomes more entrenched in his or her point of view as the proceedings move on. There is nothing any professional can do to help them make that shift. Advising a middle-aged client, for example, means dealing with someone for fifty years has been clinging to past injustices, refusing to look for resolutions and a better future. Like any habit, it's difficult to break. Additionally, there are other clients who became more entrenched in a fixed mindset because they fear change.

People are afraid of making decisions because of uncertainties. This indecision creates more doubt. This turns into fear, and the mind, for evolutionary purposes, is quite adept at putting that fear front and center in the mind, turning it into an obsession. If the indecision remains, new doubts will materialize. There are questions of how others will react to the decision.

The person becomes more and more stuck with each passing moment. People will stay in a marriage for forty years because they cannot decide what to do. These people will allow divorce proceedings to continue for years because they cannot bring themselves to sign the separation agreement.

TAKE RESPONSIBILITY

Holding yourself accountable for your role in the marriage's demise is an important part of making those decisions needed to move forward. Taking on too much responsibility is a problematic tendency that can keep someone trapped in a negative relationship.

Take the case of a husband who is unhappy, and the wife who is constantly upset with herself over her inability to make the man happier. She is taking on a responsibility that is not hers.

This man will never be happy if he is looking to someone other than himself to provide happiness. In abusive relationships, we often hear the victim excuse the violence because of it somehow being deserved. Such ownership is obviously absurd and dangerous.

People who are kidnapped sometimes have Stockholm Syndrome. This is a syndrome in which a person being held captive becomes anti-police and pro-captor.

Sometimes it takes an outsider to show the self-sacrificing spouse that sometimes owning less means owning more. Accepting responsibility for everything under the sun turns it into an empty gesture. You're certainly not helping your spouse move on by absolving him or her of any responsibility. Through soul searching, you need to locate what you're guilty of and what you're not. Moving on means unburdening yourself of this guilt.

Taking adequate and appropriate responsibility for the relationship's failure is especially crucial when children are involved. If both parents adopt this approach, they will more likely co-parent better. When parents are blaming each other, the children get pulled into the discord. They hear the griping and complaints, and soon the parents are using the children as pawns to punish or hurt the other person. When the blame game stops, the spouses can appreciate that no longer being a perfect match for marriage doesn't preclude them from being great parents together.

Think back to the original decision to have children with this other person. Try and remember the shared excitement of starting a family. Each spouse saw in each other a person worthy of this endeavor. Simply changing your perspective in this one area may be the difference between staying stuck in the mud and moving forward.

Assuming responsibility for the past goes hand in hand with seeing the good in your partner. Appreciating your spouse for whom he or she is, not to the point where you're falling in love with the person again, but to where you can fix the communication. Maybe the spouse possesses a certain charisma or is generous.

Maybe the thing that broke up the marriage is what you at one time found appealing. Your husband's work ethic impressed you until it came at the family's expense. Even if you're upset over how it damaged the marriage, you can simultaneously acknowledge the financial security and fine lifestyle gained from his hard work. Tapping into these memories will allow you to feel good about your original decision and see that it had merit. The mentality of trying to see the good in someone else is something we should bring to every encounter in life as we try to move past challenges. It's hard to stay mad at people when you can see the goodness in them.

There is also great value in adopting a more sensible approach to a partner's poorer qualities. Instead of seeing the person as thoroughly terrible, try to specifically identify the qualities that proved ruinous for the relationship. By isolating the flaws, you become more accepting of the fact that they too are on a journey, trying to do their best, and hopefully learning from any mistakes along the way.

LOSE THE VICTIM MENTALITY

If victimization enslaves you, then freeing yourself from that mindset is empowering, which is key to self-actualization. It's being able to see yourself as a powerful human being who knows your purpose and what you contribute to the world. There are people who can go through life rather effortlessly, no matter the challenges thrown their way because they have an empowering mindset. In life, you often get what you're expecting. There are people plagued with terrible beginnings to life who decide they will not allow their history to enslave them.

Oprah Winfrey was born into poverty, the daughter of a teenage single mother. In her teens, she was sexually abused and became pregnant at age fourteen. She went on to become wealthy and share her positive messages with the world.

An extreme unwillingness to take any responsibility is a sign of sociopathic or narcissistic behavior. The reflex to simply blame someone else for any misfortune while making no effort to better the situation is something deep-rooted. It is the possible result of childhood traumas, which makes it difficult behavior to change. For this person, viewing challenges from a positive point of view is near impossible. This is what I call a Charlie Brown mentality.

In the Charles M. Schulz comic strip *Peanuts*, nothing ever goes right for Charlie Brown. This is because Charlie Brown never anticipates anything ever going right. The inspirational character of the cartoon is, in fact, Snoopy. He is the only competent player on the baseball team. He possesses a rich fantasy life where he imagines himself as a fighter pilot, a famous author, and a popular college kid. He believes in possibilities and opportunities. To have any chance at a successful divorce, one needs to be like Snoopy, not Charlie Brown.

Forgiveness goes hand in hand with a positive mentality, as they are both about taking responsibility and getting past the need to be right. As Abraham Lincoln said, "Do I not destroy my enemies when I make them my friends?" This comes from a man who was known for appointing his rivals to his cabinet. A positive person doesn't have time to get bogged down in he said, she said dramas. His or her energy is focused on discovering one's purpose in the world and working to see that it comes to pass.

GRATITUDE WILL SET YOU FREE

Gratitude for all of life's experiences is another key component of this formula. This means being grateful even for all the bad moments. It means remembering people that have come into your life, those who have provided challenges and lessons that have helped you grow. Yes, this includes a bad marriage.

People get married young or get caught up in an infatuation. Soon after marrying they realize they are, in fact, opposites. The failure can help move the people forward by showing them what they do and don't want in a future relationship. Marriage is unique in that many people don't have a sense of they want at the time of tj.he union since it's not something they have ever experienced before. It's unfortunate that people can't point to this ignorance when the marriage ends and instead end up pointing the finger at the other spouse.

Gratitude will also help you get past the fear of the unknown future. When you're grateful for the smallest things in life, like being alive or having the ability to walk you can appreciate how much your mind and body can accomplish. The world is truly yours to discover.

Creating a vision for a new life is the enjoyable part of the divorce experience, but it cannot be achieved unless there is clarity of goals and wants. You need to decide, for example, if you want to enter another relationship. If so, what is the relationship going to look like? What are some of the qualities you will be looking for in a new partner? What are flaws you will look to avoid? Was there a lifestyle you were looking for in your last relationship but didn't find?

It's not simply clarity of thought. You need to imagine that it can happen to you. Anything is achievable if you truly believe it's a possibility. This is a moment for you to force yourself out of your comfort zone and create an exciting vision. Don't damage the excitement by slowly creating doubts of whether it's achievable or asking how others will receive your new path in life.

Set a course of how you will realize this vision as soon as possible. Be careful about the influences you allow into your life, people that will throw cold water on your ideas, or keep you tied to your past habits. Negative influences are all around. Sometimes the intentions of these people are good, but they themselves are fearful of the future, and they want you to share their negative, pessimistic energy.

Sadly, there are others, even friends and family, who will not want you to succeed. It pains them to watch someone get ahead of the herd. They try holding you back so that they can feel better about themselves.

Don't get sidetracked by opportunities that run counter to your plan. Loneliness is not an excuse to waist six months of your life on a relationship that you don't see as part of the future you want. A verse in Proverbs says, "Where there is no vision, the people perish."

Most people stay stuck in the routines of life, not thinking past next week. For them, visions are limited to the next planned vacations. Life has so much more to offer once you broaden your vision and match it up with the person you've discovered yourself to be through this divorce.

> *"If you're going to be thinking anything,*
> *you might as well think big."*
>
> *—Donald Trump*

CHAPTER 4

NEGOTIATING YOUR DIVORCE WITH GENEROSITY

Overcoming emotions like anger and grief and positioning oneself for a better future by adopting a growth mindset are integral to experiencing an ideal, productive divorce process. Now, we will examine why adopting an unwavering spirit of generosity is the only way to counter the unexpected twists and turns of divorce.

HOW DIVK ORCE NEGOTIATIONS SHOULD PROCEED

"Caroline"

Caroline was devastated when her husband informed her of an ongoing affair with her best friend and his plans to move in with the woman. Early in the process, this client saw that she could either choose to accept the divorce, or she could use her husband's behavior against him in hopes of attaining more favorable custody terms, a greater financial settlement and revenge.

The first hint that Caroline was not a typical client came when our lawyer witnessed how immediately receptive and accepting she was to a description of how any final divorce settlement would look regardless of her husband's infidelity. Most clients hear the term 50–50 split and automatically begin envisioning how they might be able to squeeze out a few more percentage points in their favor.

When we began discussing the issue of her children, a nine-year-old boy and a six-year-old girl, Caroline made clear her unwillingness to expose them to a nasty fight. They were ignorant of the father's misdeed, and she didn't want to tarnish the image they had of the man. Further, he was an excellent, present father, who worked hard on his relationship with the children, even after being tossed from the house.

Before lawyers got involved, they'd already begun formulating a plan to co-parent. She could see how happy the children were to spend time with him, a great example of a spouse resolving to see past the spouse's faults, by acknowledging the 'richer' aspects of the person. In the end, this was enough of a factor to get Caroline past her grief and anger. She directed me to do everything possible to swiftly reach an agreement.

> "No good marriage has ever ended in divorce."
> —*Louis CK*

What set Caroline apart from most clients was her amazing ability to compartmentalize. She mastered the high-wire balancing act of working to build a new life. She involved her husband during the negotiations so they could proceed smoothly. Too often, spouses take an all or nothing approach to the divorce, either wanting nothing to do with the spouse or being so engrossed with the negotiations that it dominates their lives and thinking.

Some participation and engagement are needed if co-parenting is going to get off on a healthy foot. Also, a spouse is going to have a hard time having his or her interests heard if he or she is absent from the process. In such cases, whenever the lawyers come back to the clients with a proposal, it doesn't reflect the clients' wishes.

Caroline wouldn't allow herself to be pulled any deeper into the process than needed. At times, her husband tried using her generosity against her, almost provoking her to become more engaged, and possibly nastier.

He insisted on lowering the amount of the projected alimony payments because the children were spending an equal amount of time at his house. This said this even though he was a wealthy man and the proposed changes would have been financially insignificant to him. When the cost of agreeing to his demands was low, she relented. When it was too high, she held her ground without letting it turn into a battle. As Kenny Rogers sang, "You've got to know when to hold me, know when to fold me."

Eventually, the case went to mediation. The parties were able to fully resolve the matter. An agreement was signed at the end of a ten-hour session. As the ink dried on the documents, the lawyers shook hands. The soon-to-be-ex spouses stood and stared at each other across the table. Short smiles broke across their faces, and they slowly stepped around the table, keeping their eyes locked on one another. They met halfway and proceeded to hug. Pulling back from the embrace, they were both teary-eyed.

This is quite an unusual ending for mediation. Usually, the parties are kept in separate rooms, and the lawyers are shuttling back and forth with offers and counteroffers. The bitterness and frustration reaching such high levels that, when the session is over, the spouses literally insist on taking separate elevators downstairs. The hugging, to me, represented this tremendous emotional moment where the parties were finally able to 'let-go'. They were cleansed, so to speak, of all the turbulence that had clouded their lives and thinking for the last year. Both had taken the high road, but Caroline's road was even higher, and it paid dividends to everyone involved, especially the children.

Although Caroline acted primarily out of the interests of her children, it ultimately benefited her, too. Some people might would argue that she could have forced her husband into a higher settlement. She did have family money belonging solely to her, which allowed her to act more positively than someone in a more financially desperate situation. Such security has not stopped other clients from using the process to exact revenge.

People like Caroline understand that holding onto anger is not healthy for the mind or body, so better to be rid of it as soon as possible. Interestingly, through an inheritance, Caroline was gifted several million dollars shortly after the separation. Maybe that's why some people believe in karma.

If this windfall had occurred while they were still legally married, she may have had to share some of it with the husband. The timing worked out because she ran out the clock. When couples are busy fighting over a divorce, they are blind to all the potential opportunities coming in and out of their lives. This creates a chance to start a new relationship, a new hobby, a new life.

START FROM A POSITION OF GENEROSITY

Generosity is key to a positive divorce and a fruitful existence. You should always under promise and over deliver in everything you do. The wealthiest people in the world are not wealthy because they are the scrooges of the world. They arrive at their success by being generous and showing a willingness to share. This ultimately opens them up to other people and possibilities. Who doesn't want to spend time around generous people?

In the context of a divorce, generosity should not make you poor, but you should remain open to the likelihood that giving a little can go a long way. Clients, too often, see everything in black and white terms. They might be unwilling to deviate, even slightly, from some rules established at the outset. "She will never see a dime from the business."

People end up taking extreme positions because most of life resides in grayer shades, which makes them extremely difficult to navigate. When issues are gray, people must be willing to bend on principals and values to get what they want. It's unrealistic to think you can deal solely in black and white positions. You will have to make a compromise.

In a divorce, everyone is eventually forced to sign a document, unless you're willing to go to prison for contempt of court. Better you determine early in the process to take the big picture and consider what result you can live with while keeping in mind the monetary and emotional cost of any protracted battle.

Being cheap always comes with a cost, a sacrifice. Buy cheap shoes, and they will need resoling in six months. People go through a long, nasty court battle full of accusations and name-calling expecting that after the judgment is handed down, they'll be able to simply tuck away the last year or two as if nothing happened. The wounds opened during a lengthy battle may never heal. Depression is real and dangerous. People can die because of a divorce.

The need for generosity is not limited to matters of money and custody. It extends to questions of forgiveness and acceptance. By adopting a generous spirit, you're declaring that you'll not get bogged down by the past and are willing to do what is needed to move forward. It's also acknowledging that you don't stand in judgment of the spouse and his or her contribution to the marriage's demise.

You accept the other person and don't feel that he or she deserves to suffer any more than you do or pay a certain price to gain redemption. Hopefully, this will earn you mileage with the spouse in the long run. Nobody wants to feel they are being judged. Your spouse wants to be accepted as an equal. They don't walk around feeling as if he or she has disappointed you. Demanding someone beg for forgiveness is evil. It's another example of playing the victim.

The golden rule is an excellent inspiration when it comes to resolving any conflict. "Do unto others as you would have them do unto you." This can be framed in many other ways. I will think about this person the way I want them thinking about me. I will judge them as a parent in the way I'd want them judging me. Finally, I'm going to treat my spouse through this process, the way I want my spouse to treat me.

The golden rule is unconditional. The other spouse's behavior no matter how poor doesn't cancel out the golden rule. Getting to this level of thinking will allow you to eliminate anger. It will certainly allow for more constructive conversation. Divorce provides you with an opportunity to cultivate that level of thinking so that you can bring it to all aspects of your life. This will pull you out of conflicts and away from the fear and uncertainty they carry with them.

It can be crystal clear that the other person is in the wrong. All your family and friends confirm your stance. On some level, however, you must recognize that hanging on to these feelings are not productive. Righteousness isn't going to undo the past.

KEEPING THE LINES OF COMMUNICATION OPEN

Communication is the foundation of all relationships, so it's natural that this is the area where a spirit of generosity will face its greatest test. Ideally, couples will be on speaking terms during divorce. This doesn't mean they need to discuss substantial issues relating to the settlement. After all, there may be an underlying issue of bullying, or a power imbalance in the relationship or the divorce may still be too raw for one of the parties. Obviously, in such instances, couples should not negotiate matters pertaining to the divorce. But spouses will never get to the point of forgiveness or move on if they can't even have a civil conversation about the weather. If they can't make small talk, how will they deal with the many parenting disagreements that will surely arise?

Does a father want to take a child to a movie deemed inappropriate by the mother? Does the mother want to enroll a child in a certain activity against the wishes of a father? Some people will feast on these moments as another opportunity to fight. If you have decided to operate with a spirit of generosity, you need to consider how you will navigate these potentially thorny issues.

The key is to take a step back and ask how you can approach the matter in the most generous way possible. If you can't trust yourself to conduct a fruitful conversation or communication has broken down completely, then look to outside resources to help facilitate constructive discussions. Mediation is a good example.

If needed, a parenting coordinator, usually a licensed mental health or legal professional appointed by the court, can meet with the couple. They will listen to their respective positions on any given matter. They will issue a binding decision that can only be challenged by a court motion. This latter option is obviously not ideal, but it's preferable to two spouses raising tensions by speaking disrespectfully to one another and allowing communication to further deteriorate.

If communication with your current spouse is a problem area, you need to work on this issue before moving on to a new relationship. Don't assume communication will suddenly improve with a different partner. A healthy, strong line of communication typically says more about you than the other person.

Communication breaks down when the other person feels as if they aren't being heard and respected. If you can generously accept that whatever is coming out of the other person's mouth is his or her truth, even if you think it's patently false, then you will have a greater chance of getting your point across to the other person.

Fear is what drives most poor communication. People fear not getting what they want, so they put up barriers that prevent proper communication. It's important to recognize that your own thoughts don't require outside validation to be considered legitimate.

A deep belief in this idea will liberate you to speak authentically. It will free you from judgments. It will also prevent you from being angry the second the other person rejects your thoughts. Take the example of someone in a work meeting who raises his hand and voices a suggestion that is quickly laughed at by everyone in the room.

Chances are the reaction will make him feel stupid. He will think twice about raising his hand the next time. But if he took a generous approach towards himself, accepted the possibility that their criticism is what was wrong, then he'd have no trouble raising his hand the next time he wanted to share.

Sometimes a lawyer will instruct a client to avoid communication regarding contentious issues, but this doesn't mean the couple should not try discussing more positive subjects in hopes of fostering a healthy, pleasant relationship. In general, it's preferable that spouses communicate face-to-face and not through letters or phone calls.

The same is true of lawyers. Body language, as we dealt with in the previous chapter, can tell you whether the other person is speaking authentically and stands behind his or her comments. I remember seeing a quote along the lines of, "People believe verbal language 50 percent of the time, but they believe body language 99 percent of the time."

Judges have the task of determining a witness's credibility and have to study body language as part of their training. There is also an energy that transpires between people in face-to-face meetings. From the energy emanating from the other person, one can surmise what is important to the other person, whether the parties are receptive to each other's positions and, most importantly, if the other side is negotiating out of generosity or malice.

In our day and age, face-to-face communication is complicated by our over-reliance on technology, specifically, social media. We fail to appreciate how much is lost when we converse through typing. People may misinterpret a short email as rude, or misread a sarcastic comment written by a lawyer hoping to lighten the mood.

A lawyer might send the opposing counsel a five-page letter with his or her thoughts on the case. The other lawyer will more likely than not interpret the document as the other side's fixed positions, even if they are just general thoughts. In turn, he or she will feel a need to respond, and the two positions will quickly become entrenched. Therefore, when a face-to-face meeting is not possible, a phone call is the preferable alternative.

The written word does have an important place in law. When all is said and done, the agreement will be written down. If a challenge is ever brought, a judge will look at the words, not the litigants' body language. But the written word should happen at the end of the process. At most, during the negotiations, lawyers should write down only the points of agreement so that each party can verify the language. Lawyers, however, should not engage in long correspondence. All messages should be short, sweet, and to the point.

THE CHILDREN STAND TO LOSE THE MOST

It should come as no surprise that divorce has the potential to have consequences on children. The greatest benefit you stand to attain by pledging a spirit of generosity is the increased likelihood that you will secure a more positive for your children.

Studies suggest that children of divorce turn to drugs or suffer from eating disorders. They might achieve poor academic results in greater numbers than children who grow up in two-parent homes. This is no surprise given that divorce leaves many children feeling rejected. Some go as far as taking responsibility for the marriage's collapse.

Paul Amato, an American sociologist, shows from his own research that most of the negative costs are not a result of the children suffering through a conflict-ridden marriage, or even the actual separation itself. Rather, the cause is 'the accumulation of subsequent family transitions that divorce often sets into motion'. In other words, the greatest potential trauma lies in the resulting chaos triggered by the divorce.[6]

Children of divorce suddenly feel as if they are put in the middle of the conflict. They feel pressure to prove to both parents that they love them equally. They don't want to take sides. Hurting a parent's feelings becomes a constant concern.

Typically, the less money a couple has, the more they fight over the children. Someone is angry, or grief-stricken, and the children become a convenient way of hurting the spouse. Custody disputes are, in fact, rare with wealthy clients.

Often, the child of divorce feels the loss more than the parents. In most cases, the child may be aware of constant tension between his or her mother and father. The parents have tried to protect the child by keeping secret any discussions about divorce. Therefore the announcement comes as a shock to the child.

It's almost like the difference between someone dying of cancer versus a person dropping dead from a sudden heart attack. Add to this shock the fear of having no concept of how this future family will look. Some children will never lose hope that their parents will end up back together. When the parent meets someone new, sometimes years after the divorce, the child might not be able to accept the new partner because of this longing to recreate the past.

At the time of the divorce, children experience, even more than loss, a sense of isolation, or loneliness. The support system they have come to rely on until now appears to have collapsed overnight. Children need support to feel secure both emotionally and financially. Parents are a child's constant in life. It's the thing they know they will always come home to. When a parent removes him or herself from the home, the child scrambles to find a replacement. Sometimes the replacement might be a gang, alcohol, or drugs.

To fill the void, the child will retreat inwards via video games or some other obsession. The pain is felt even more sharply when they feel particularly close to the parent that moved out. It's crucial, therefore, for the child to feel that both parents will love him or her no matter the outcome. The love must feel unconditional.

When a child witnesses generosity towards the other parent, it's a signal to him or her that the center is holding. With this constant firmly in place, the child will feel safe enough to move forward and will feel better about any risks the parents may make in attempting a better future, for example, finding a new partner. If the parent is angry, doing everything to frantically hold on to the other parent, it sends the opposite message.

A child at the age of five, ten, or fifteen should be exploring the world, not feeling its weight. Yet, parents or the family court will put children in a position to make decisions about how the family will look moving forward. These parents are doing nothing less than passing on responsibilities to their children. These couples can't understand that a child's love is so great that he or she will do anything to not hurt the parent. The child is even willing to live out of a suitcase.

Parents need to accept the responsibility of coming up with a parenting plan themselves, instead of asking the child to make one for them. In some situations, a mother will say that the child asked to stay with her, and the father will turn right back and respond that the child made the same comment to him.

Do they not hear that the child is simply telling both what they want to hear? Could they not anticipate these types of consequences before making the decision to divorce? If you're struggling to find a reason to assume a spirit of generosity, look no further than your children. More than anything, children want their parents' love. Adopting this approach is the opportunity to show them you're putting them first.

CHAPTER 5

FINDING THE LAWYER WHO IS YOUR PERFECT MATCH

The less negativity you have in your divorce, the less you will bring into your new life, which includes the future relationship with your ex-spouse. Kindness, therefore, is crucial throughout the divorce proceedings. Kindness, in fact, is a cure for all conflicts. As the saying goes, "Kill them with kindness." This doesn't mean you should act like a dog that gets hit and then comes back for another beating. Like everything in life, finding the right balance is important.

Still, if someone wrongs you, raising the ante by exacting revenge is more likely to start a vicious cycle and deepen the enmity than prove productive. If in the moment you don't have it in you to act kindly, then heed the Bible's warning to turn the other cheek. In other words, at the very least, don't engage. The New Testament's ideas of forgiveness and loving your enemy, in my opinion, marks a progression from the Old Testament's justice of an eye for an eye. If you're trading an eye for an eye and a tooth for a tooth back and forth with your nemesis, you and your enemy will be left with no eyes or teeth.

This futility of hatred recalls the ending of West Side Story. After Tony is killed, Maria, his lover, holds him in her arms. As the rival gangs are about to violently engage each other once more, Maria grabs the gun off the floor and uses it to draw them back. She says, "You all killed him… Not with bullets and guns. With hate! Well, I can kill, too, because now I have hate!"

Most people eventually figure out how to move forward with the divorce. The pity is that it takes the loss of significant time and money to reach this conclusion. Therefore kindness must inform your choice in a legal team, as well as your choice in a therapist and financial advisor.

FINDING THE RIGHT LAWYER

Kindness, for many lawyers, is not a factor in how they practice family law. Instead, they adopt a mechanical, impersonal attitude that has them talking about precedents and legal rights the moment the client takes a seat in the office. They believe the information helps the client feel in control of their situation.

It does stir the client up, but often to a detrimental effect, encouraging both parties to become fixated on the question of what they are 'entitled to'. All the energy and emotions go into fighting over which one gets the kids on national holidays. This leaves little energy to work on fostering a better relationship with the other side. Engrossed with the bricks and mortars, they fail to consider the interior design.

It may take time to find a lawyer who is supportive of a client taking a kind approach, but it will be well worth the effort. First, you will save money and time by not having a drawn-out divorce. Second, you will rid yourself of the emotional pain sooner. With the backing of a team operating out of kindness, you will be forced to engage your spouse as the person you once loved, and not someone you now detest.

The process will become the forum for you to immediately begin establishing a healthy relationship with the soon-to-be ex-spouse. Third, you must consider that like a pebble falling into water, divorce has a tangible ripple effect on the people in your life. We know divorce is hard on children, but it will also be painful for your parents. Chances are they are elderly, and it will take an emotional toll on them to see you undergo such a tumultuous episode. Or consider how the divorce will dominate your thoughts, pushing work matters to the side. Your employer will tolerate a preoccupied employee for so long.

ARE LAWYERS EVEN NECESSARY

Someone determined to act out of kindness may think that a lawyer is unnecessary. Twenty-three years ago, 10% of family law litigants were unrepresented, meaning they represented themselves. Now, 70% of people in Toronto Canada represent themselves in family court. This has obviously led to a huge loss of business for lawyers, who have not reacted to this change by looking for ways to lower the costs of the average divorce, which is the major driver of this change. Therefore ClearWay Law offers self-represented coaching.

Overall, I believe, this trend of people taking on divorce without a lawyer is a negative one. In cases of unrepresented litigants, judges are forced to take on a greater role, acting as lawyers for the parties. In recent years, in fact, courts of appeal have overturned some of the decisions in these cases. They said that arguing that the judges went too far in assisting the unrepresented. This is especially common in cases where one spouse is represented, and the other is not. This is a situation that compels the judge to act almost like the unrepresented person's advocate.

Another reason for this drift, in addition to the money issue, is that thanks to the tremendous resources available on the internet, people feel they can do it on their own. Ultimately, however, they don't do a good job. It takes years of training and experience to have a solid handle on the main issues— small and large— that go into negotiating a divorce.

There was a sophisticated client whom our lawyers counseled to represent himself. He was acting generously and was going up against an aggressive lawyer, the type of counsel judges like to tell to sit down. The client ran the eight-day trial on his own and won. This was a rare situation, and most of the time people don't have a full sense of what they are doing.

Self-represented people almost always lose if the other side has a lawyer. Therefore self-represented coaching is important.

Lawyers aren't often needed in the following situations:

- ▲ In a situation where the couple has only been together for three or four years
- ▲ The couple have little to no assets
- ▲ There are no children
- ▲ The spouses have close to equal standards of income and assets
- ▲ They want to move on in their lives as quickly as possible

In almost all cases, however, a lawyer is needed at some point during the divorce. Normally this is just a separation agreement or some independent legal advice.

WHAT MAKES A GOOD LAWYER

The ideal lawyer-client relationship is one where the lawyer feels almost like a teacher. He assesses a client's situation in a personal manner, allowing for a give and take. This is different than an approach that treats all divorces and clients as equal problems with equal solutions. A good lawyer is someone who has plenty of experience, allowing him or her to come up with solutions and ideas for compromise that a client never would have thought on his or her own.

There are a multitude of creative ways to solve disputes surrounding money and children that can allow both parties to feel as if they came out on top. Creativity will only flow from a lawyer with years of experience and a desire to deal out of kindness. A good, considerate lawyer will also lessen the emotional load by making sure you're in the right frame of mind and putting your fears to rest.

Skill and experience are essential when it comes time to drafting a solid separation agreement that will stand the test of time by anticipating future challenges. There are many ways to attack agreements if they are not worded or structured correctly and leave things open to interpretation. There are many ways to make an agreement more enforceable. Therefore you need a lawyer to do your agreement.

Facilitating and easing communication between the spouses is another valuable service provided by a good lawyer. Part of the reason the marriage broke down is because the spouses lost their ability to communicate properly and effectively. The lawyer can sit down his or her client and encourage them to talk to the spouse and help establish boundaries of what is acceptable conversation. Maybe the couple can discuss the children's progress in school, or work to be done in the house.

The important thing is to keep the conversation within the boundaries and allow the lawyers to discuss the divorce proceedings and the more complicated issues. This is a great way for the couple to start parenting together without the worry that it will devolve into arguments better left to lawyers. You're going to have to have a decent relationship at some point to successfully co-parent, so you might as well start now.

"This is the part where you find out who you are."

Whether someone needs a lawyer or not for the duration of the process depends on the state of your relationship between the spouses. If the couple is still on friendly terms and a power balance between them is not present, then they can sit down and work together on an agreement without lawyers, provided they take the time to educate themselves on rights and precedents.

There are plenty of books that can help these couples, as well as wonderful resources on the internet. In fact, many lawyers post a large amount of information on their websites. A lawyer is recommended if the parties don't have the time to familiarize themselves with the many issues surrounding divorce— division of assets, child support, alimony, custody— or if the relationship has soured and they can no longer effectively communicate.

The question of needing a lawyer isn't an all or nothing approach. Even if you can resolve two-thirds of the issues without fighting before you meet with lawyers, you'll have saved a substantial amount of time, money, energy, and stress.

Self-awareness plays an important role in making this decision. There are situations where one spouse may try bullying the other into not hiring a lawyer and wrapping up the matter as quickly as possible. Perhaps the concern is money, or maybe he or she is conscious of an ability to intimidate the other person.

Know that many lawyers provide an initial consultation free of charge. I would recommend against this. They are often just sales meetings. It's better to pay a discounted rate for a lawyer's time and get a full hour of actual legal advice.

Plenty of lawyers will try to rile you up so they can get a costly divorce or try and convince you that you must protect your rights and not let up for a second. A good lawyer will help you think through the makeup of the relationship with the spouse and if not having counsel is an advantageous plan for you.

When Jenny came into our firm for a consultation, she revealed that her husband was quite insistent that they not use lawyers. I quickly learned that he ran a successful private company. The husband claimed that any scrutiny of his business would be an unnecessary additional stress to him, the company, and the assets they would be dividing. This reluctance to have his wife's lawyer digging through his financial records was, for me, a giant red flag. This was a woman in need of legal advice from one of our lawyers.

You should contact a family lawyer right away if:

- ⋏   The assets are spread out in multiple accounts
- ⋏   You don't understand how much money and assets you have
- ⋏   One spouse is the beneficiary of a significant trust
- ⋏   You are locked out of the bank account

It doesn't mean the divorce must turn contentious. There is no reason the lawyers from both sides, with the assistance of financial planners, cannot work in a cooperative, collaborative manner to creatively untangle the finances and minimize the taxes that come with transferring assets.

Crafting a divorce agreement is not rocket science. In a long-term marriage, everything might be divided fifty-fifty. The support payments are straightforward, and the parenting plans will call for the children to spend substantial amounts of time with both parents. A couple spending tens, sometimes hundreds, of thousands of dollars fighting to get to what will eventually be an even split is a bad decision. The money would be put to better use on the children's future.

Finding the lawyer that is the right fit for you should be a thoughtful, deliberative process. Referrals from colleagues or family members are an excellent place to start your search, but you should accept all recommendations with a degree of caution. A person may sing the praises of a lawyer simply because he or she is pleased with the lawyer's aggressiveness and willingness to destroy the other spouse. You can begin vetting the lawyer by doing research on the internet. Most lawyers will post their values and outlook on their firm's webpage.

You can see my law firm's values at www.clearwaylaw.com.

A quick scan of this readily available information can tell you whether the lawyer is one who takes a more holistic approach of divorce and will seek to minimize your emotional scars, or if he or she will tie your life up in litigation for the next year and a half.

Eventually, you need to take the time to become familiar with the lawyer's philosophy and temperament and to see whether it matches your criteria. Interview the lawyer. Treat it like a job interview and get a sense of the lawyer's style. Ask how he or she approaches the practice of law, whether he or she has experience in cases like yours and, if so, how the matters were ultimately prosecuted and resolved. Normally you can get a cheap rate for the first hour of time.

You can get a sense of how the lawyer will approach the case strategically, and if this aligns with how you conduct negotiations and dialogue in your own life. If you're not a highly combative person in your everyday life, you should not be made to feel that somehow divorce is unique, and you need to change your personal style to achieve success. A clash with your lawyer down the road can mean having to wage a two-front battle against your lawyer and spouse.

At the end of the day, you must feel as if the lawyer is hearing you, and that he or she knows what is important to you. This is different to the lawyer who is eager to start the process and makes blanket, impersonal assumptions of what is right for your case. A lawyer who never asks about your ultimate goals and the place you want to be emotionally and materially at the end of the divorce is a lawyer who is not listening. Be wary of the lawyer who talks more than you at the initial meeting. Don't be shy to ask straight out if he or she understands what is important to you.

From that first consultation, you will be able to tell whether the lawyer is trying to help you or merely sell you something. One of my associates, for example, doesn't permit potential clients to retain her at the introductory meeting. She talks about her process and philosophy. Most importantly, she listens.

At the end of the hour, she tells the person to go home and think about whether they are a good fit or not. On the other end of the spectrum are the lawyers who are trying to get clients to sign on the dotted line ten minutes after stepping foot into the office. Some clients want to find a lawyer right away.

Another point to keep in mind is that you will need a lawyer even if you choose to shape an agreement without representation. Have you managed to work through one hundred percent of the issues with your spouse? A lawyer is still required for the writing of the settlement or separating agreement. Don't use an online template as they are not tailored to your unique situation.

People do a poor job of drafting these documents themselves, even when using a template downloaded from the internet. There are many ways lawyers, later down the road, can open these agreements and argue the legitimacy of certain provisions. Perhaps your friends today with the spouse. Hopefully, it remains that way forever. You want to prepare for the possibility of a soured relationship. Maybe the spouse gets jealous when you enter a new relationship. Maybe someone whispers something into his or her ear about not getting a fair shake in the agreement. Hiring lawyers to basically sign off on the agreement doesn't have to be costly. Most separation agreements cost around $3500 (Canadian dollars) to finalize.

The two of you can share the cost of hiring a lawyer to prepare any documents that will have integrity and be protected from future court applications, and then each of you can hire a separate, personal lawyer to review the document. Then, the lawyer can be on hand to witness the document's signing. Sometimes one partner waives the right to independent legal advice.

People often don't enter the process with a good sense of their legal rights. Take the case of a mother who claims that the workaholic father is never home at night to put the children to bed. The father has not once has taken the time to come to a soccer match. She may come into the divorce assuming she will automatically receive physical and residential custody of the children. The court might determine each spouse is entitled to equal time.

It may not sound fair to the mother, but that is the law. She also needs to understand that just because he has been absent until now doesn't mean he will not be a good, single parent when forced into the role. Or a case in which the husband builds a business from the ground up, and he is surprised to learn that the courts see the wife as an equal owner of the company. Lawyers help educate you about what a family law judge might decide.

Movies show that it's always the man that pays support to the women. It's not true.

He may have difficulty accepting the argument that she was the one who cared for the children and home. This enabled him to pursue his business with minimal distractions. Or sometimes wives don't understand that they are the ones who must pay alimony in cases where they earn more than their husbands. In all these examples, and many more, lawyers can prove useful in dashing people's assumptions and setting them straight on law and rights.

More women are working spouses and changes in the law are beginning to reflect that shift. If a woman is thirty-five years old and has, until now, been a stay-at-home mom, the court is unlikely to grant her alimony for the rest of her life. It will simply provide time for her to get the education and training she needs to find a job and build the foundation of a career. The law now imposes an obligation on both spouses to become self-supporting. Getting married to a rich person is not a lifelong meal ticket.

Interpersonal skills are obviously a crucial factor when selecting a lawyer. Therefore a face-to-face meeting is critically important. So much of communication takes place through body language rather than words. You can look in someone's face and tell whether effective communication is happening. Is he or she looking you in the eyes as you both speak?

Does he or she speak in a threatening or over-aggressive manner? Is the person's body inching closer to you as he or she talks? Is the person comfortable, or is he or she fidgety, maybe rocking his or her foot or chewing on a pen? You can tell quickly from a person's tone and the way they comport themselves whether he or she is a nurturing and caring person. A lawyer who is academically sharp, but has a poor bedside manner is not one I would choose.

In family law, EQ, emotional quotient or intelligence, is almost more important than IQ, intelligence quotient. Family law is not complicated tax or securities issues being litigated. What is important in a lawyer is the ability to understand and manage clients' emotions and keep the opposing side equally calm. Therefore family law is unique.

External factors like the lawyer's dress and office should also be factors when deciding. This person will be meeting with your spouse's lawyer and possibly standing in a court of law. He or she will not make a good first impression by showing up with a dirty suit and unkempt hair.

It suggests disorganization in the lawyer's life. A professional atmosphere where the office staff answers your questions and treats you respectfully will help contribute to a smoother process all around. At a time of great stress in your life, you don't need additional anxieties like wrongly scheduled appointments, lost files, and unreturned phone calls.

If you've just endured an emotionally draining hour-long meeting with your lawyer, you don't want to have to stick around for twenty minutes to have your parking validated.

Some people go through two or three lawyers over the course of a family dispute. A client may think he or she wants a lawyer who will destroy the other side only to discover once negotiations begin that the anger has dissipated, and a harmonious process is now desired. If you decide to terminate your lawyer, you need to think whether you're doing so for a valid reason.

Too often, clients become angry with lawyers because the advice and decisions are not providing emotional satisfaction. This says more about the client than it does the lawyer. It's an indication that the client is still holding on to feelings of anger or grief, and what's needed is, not a new lawyer, but more counseling, because anyone can bet correctly that this client will end up changing lawyers again and end up just as dissatisfied.

Another red flag is a lawyer who boasts over how much experience he or she has in arguing trials. The question to ask this lawyer is why he or she cannot seem to settle matters outside the courtroom. Is the lawyer is bragging from the outset about the many trials won? This is a strong indication that you will one day get to see the inside of a courtroom.

Lawyers do have the power to fuel a conflict by how they communicate in person and through writing with other lawyers. One strong sentence in a letter is enough to fire up the spouse and her legal team. You want a lawyer who has experience in the courtroom yet boasts of the many cases settled through mediation and arbitration.

At the end of the day, the lawyer you choose should see him or herself as a helping professional who brings specialized knowledge to the situation. He or she should be looking to help the family transition to a new type of family in an efficient and less destructive way. Protecting your money should not be his or her only task. Mental health should be of an even greater concern since that will determine the richness of your life after the divorce.

Divorce is a tremendously difficult time for people. The lawyer is not a therapist, but he or she can determine whether therapy is needed and if it's proving effective. A lawyer should look to unburden the client of any emotional anguish, and not increase the person's anxiety by not returning phone calls or fueling the conflict and enmity between the spouses. Most importantly, a lawyer's job is to make sure you and your entire team are acting out of kindness and compassion, the way we all hope to be treated as we journey through this life.

Clients need to know that lawyers have multiple clients, court dates, and life demands. Lawyers need time to respond to client questions.

CHAPTER 6

MAKING YOUR DIVORCE
SHORT AND SWEET

Divorce will never be fun. No one is happy to have to hire ClearWay Law. Who likes paying a lawyer?

Even if you and your spouse have worked past any destructive emotions, adopted a generous spirit, and embraced the possibility of a better future, the best you can hope for is a smooth divorce that doesn't wipe out your life savings or hurt your children emotionally. There is a good possibility of bad things happening if both parties enter the process wanting to hurt the other person. It's when spouses function reactively, instead of responsively, that the process risks spiraling out of control.

WHAT IS THE RIGHT THING TO DO?

Most people go through life reacting to other people's words and actions. Someone says something they don't like, and they must answer right away, and put the person in his or her place. They never stop to consider that the comeback will only increase the tension. They fail to take the time to contemplate an appropriate response and determine whether it's the best course of action. Telling someone off, or speaking one's mind, may bring a feeling of euphoria. This is usually a momentary high, a rush of adrenaline, that comes at the high cost of continued conflict, long-term anguish, and angst.

It may take therapy or counseling to help you gain control of your emotions and to think more clearly. But if you succeed, there is no question, it will mean a life of less hysteria and better results. If your spouse sends you a nasty text or leaves a hostile message on your voicemail, don't feel the need to respond immediately. It will only increase the tension. In the morning, email or call your lawyer and discuss an appropriate response. Remember, the goal at the end of the day is to reach a resolution, not to prove you're right.

A great leader is someone who calms the emotions of the people and shows them a different path forward, not the person who follows an emotional tide thirsting for revenge. Vicious cycles of anger, bitterness, and violence are what drive up the costs of all battles. Nobody looks back with pride at the moments where they allowed emotions, instead of logic, to govern them. All they see is waste, devastation, and missed opportunities. Think of instances in your own life where you may have reacted rashly in a rude or inconsiderate manner. The guilt is sometimes punishing enough, but then comes the torment of trying to figure out how you're going to make things right again.

WORST-CASE SCENARIO

Teale

Consider the case of Teale, one of the most 'reactionary' clients that our law firm had to deal with, and one whose divorce got out of hand in a hurry. She would come into ClearWay Law and report on a series of exchanges between her and her husband. In her accounts, she was always the victim of her husband's evil behavior. She would write letters— against her lawyers' advice— listing all the ways he failed her and the children. He would answer the charges in an equally hostile note. They would go up and back. This wasn't communication designed to foster understanding and resolution. In fact, from the way she described her letters, it was clear her intention was to hurt her husband and make him feel low. She needed him to know that he was a bad, bad man.

I would talk to her about the need to take a break from communicating with him until she gained better control of her emotions and could deal with him in a constructive, and not destructive, manner. Any break in communication would last for a couple of weeks until a small comment or perceived slight was taken by her an opportunity to re-engage with the husband.

A child leaving her retainer at home when she went to the father's house turned into a screed about him being an irresponsible and inconsiderate man. A supposed glance at her when he dropped off the children was turned into one of the most disrespectful gestures anyone has ever made at her. She would overreact to every slight criticism. He would toss a pebble at her, and she'd feel she had to fight back with everything she had.

She believed her children would be fine if they never saw their father again. The children eventually became estranged from the man. For months, I worked with Teale and the husband's team on a reunification plan. We involved some of the top counselors in the area. While we negotiated, Teale worked tirelessly on destroying any progress in the divorce.

She would find problems with the counselors or say things to the children, which would result in them taking a negative approach to the process. At times, when we discussed the matter, she could intellectually appreciate the benefit reunification would have for the children.

She couldn't take herself out of the equation, so the entire reunification plan became about her, and not the children. The husband wasn't perfect, but he had that desire to make it work for the sake of the children. This want was lacking in her. The process eventually failed, which is an extremely rare occurrence.

She and the husband settled days before the trial was set to begin. Teale received a routine settlement, one that she would have gotten through mediation or arbitration a year earlier at a fraction of the cost. To this day, she feels as though she didn't get the justice she felt she deserved. The court didn't acknowledge her as a saint who had to put up with a devil.

Teale is a highly sensitive person who cannot let things roll off her back, and she is still fighting with her ex-husband about visitation rights and support payments. The children suffered greatly. All three have serious behavioral and social issues. Naturally, when I talk to Teale about counseling for the children, she insists they are doing well and adjusting smoothly. In her world, nothing positive is being created or accomplished.

At the end of the day, despite the bleak outcome, I like to believe that our lawyers succeeded in minimizing the damage. On plenty of occasions, the lawyers managed to talk Teale off the cliff, preventing her from muddying the waters even more. With a different lawyer, I am confident she would have gone to trial and spent even more money. In a tongue in cheek way, I view Teale's case as an inspirational tale. If a client like her could avoid trial and its exorbitant cost, so can anyone. The challenge is finding an alternative avenue suited to the specific marriage and the unique interests of the spouses involved.

THERE ARE ALTERNATIVES

Keeping lawyers out of the actual negotiations is preferable whenever possible. Most lawyers are hardwired to win, making every small a battle. This outlook doesn't leave room for compromise, a mindset that is particularly dangerous when there are custody issues at stake. If one of the lawyers and his side are winning, then chances are the children stand to become the biggest losers when it's all done.

ONE-ON-ONE

Negotiating one-on-one, therefore, is a worthwhile avenue to explore, provided the lines of communication between spouses are open and void of any bullying or power imbalance. It will only work if both spouses are open to each other's perspectives and interests and don't see the marriage as a failure, but a slight misstep in life's long journey.

If the assets are rather straightforward, you and your spouse should be able to sit down at the kitchen table with all the statements from your various financial institutions and come to a fair agreement. If you own property, you can speak to a real estate agent about how much it is worth. In my four years in the family law industry, I have only seen several disputes where the parties couldn't divide up the home's personal furnishings.

Usually, each spouse wants specific items. If you find you and your spouse are fighting over who gets the wedding albums, then one-on-one negotiations might not be the right alternative for you. When there are items that neither party wants or are of no use, then the simple solution is to sell the items and split any money earned on the sale.

Generally, a lawyer will add up the division of assets. If the husband is set to receive $600,000 worth of assets and the wife gets $400,000, then the husband will pay her a $100,000 equalization payment.

Relatively intelligent people can crunch these numbers on their own, but if it proves too difficult, you can hire an accountant for a cost far lower than hiring a lawyer. In any agreement, proper designations should be in place for life insurance. Think about making the other spouse the beneficiary since it's he or she who will end up having sole responsibility of the children's care.

For most jurisdictions, online calculators are available to help assist in determining spousal support. Plug in the parties' income, length of the marriage, ages of the children, and other pertinent information, and the calculator will provide a range of options. Be warned that determining this number becomes complicated when one party is self-employed and doesn't have a fixed income. In such a situation, an accountant or lawyer may be able to provide creative solutions.

It's important to think through every issue that has the potential to turn into a major conflict down the road. What if the father, for example, has custody of the young children over the weekend, but occasionally must work on Sundays. The parties need to agree on what is considered suitable childcare. You don't want a situation where months later the wife finds out that the former-sister-in-law, who she detests, and thinks is irresponsible, is watching the children.

Even in cases where the couple gets along well, a tremendous amount of detail needs to be contained in the separation agreement. For instance, the couple should negotiate how they will decide a child's extracurricular activities and who will be responsible for its cost. How should child support payments be adjusted once the child goes off to university? What if the child decides on pursuing a secondary degree? There are plenty of resources online to learn about rights, guidelines, and responsibilities in cases of divorce.

If some of the above issues prove difficult to negotiate, don't hesitate to involve a lawyer. They have many solutions at their fingertips and can always recommend a parenting coordinator. A child specialist can help sort through these issues and make sure you're approaching the matter from a counseling perspective rather than a legal one.

Even in an ideal situation where the parties can sit down at the kitchen table and effortlessly hammer out an agreement, a lawyer should be retained when the couple is ready to put it down in writing. This is money well spent.

I can't emphasize enough the importance of each spouse retaining independent legal counsel before the process is completed. Lawyers possess the skills to evaluate the agreement and to sharpen the language where needed, so there are no challenges or fights down the road.

MEDIATION

There are people who despite possessing a growth mindset and a desire to start a new life cannot handle one-on-one negotiations with their spouses. Maybe a lack of confidence has them afraid to raise certain topics. They don't yet possess the objectivity to fully appreciate the other side's interests. Some people cannot physically or emotionally handle the immense research and work an unrepresented negotiation entail. Thankfully, for these people, there are other options for negotiating an affordable divorce.

Mediation has emerged as a popular resolution process for divorce. The risk of lawyers further fueling the conflict automatically lessens when a neutral third party is inserted into the negotiations. An experienced mediator with a legal background acts as a reality check. They offer an opinion on what has been negotiated up until that point.

He or she can speak frankly with lawyers and keep them in line and tell them when they are making unreasonable demands. Through dialogue, a mediator can quickly tell when a lawyer is advocating an extreme position that is not aligned with the client's viewpoint and interests. A seasoned mediator facilitates a more objective discussion that will ultimately bring the spouses closer together in their thinking.

Mediation works because it is a process. The mediator doesn't have the authority to impose a decision. Traditionally, the mediation takes an entire day, but after a few hours— usually spent by the mediator going between the two parties— the lawyers and mediator have an outline of the eventual settlement. The rest of the day is about getting the spouses emotionally ready to sign. The mediator accomplishes this by allowing both spouses to be heard. This is the thing people want most out of the process. They want their pain and the perceived injustices acknowledged. Lawyers, after all, have the tendency overwhelm their clients.

Due to email correspondence and lawyers instructing their clients to not speak directly to the other spouse, a client may feel as if he or she is not being heard. The mediator will often silence the lawyers and ask to hear directly from both spouses. This enables the mediator to get a better handle on what the spouses are thinking and feeling. For the clients, mediation becomes their day in court, and the mediator is the merciful judge who helps them understand that we are all human.

Once the spouses feel that they were heard, they begin to understand the finite options available to resolve the conflict. They start to appreciate the value of concluding the matter by the end of the day and not spending any more money on the divorce. These various exercises conducted throughout the day are helping the parties let go of the fight. The need to compromise is eventually appreciated. They may not end up arriving at their ideal situation, but they'll reach an agreement they truly feel they can accept.

During the mediation, with the mediator spending half of his or her time with the other party, a lawyer spends a significant amount of alone time with the client. It's good to use this time to encourage a positive, upbeat mindset in the client by talking about exciting possibilities for the future and how free he or she will feel at the end of the mediation when all of this is behind him or her. Instead of trash talking the other lawyer and spouse, a lawyer should talk up their good qualities, tell the client that the lawyer seems like a fair man. The lawyer might say that the other spouse is an excellent parent. It's about creating an atmosphere of positivity. The client feels as if that moment is the diving line between a hellish past and a blissful future.

With mediation, lawyers are free to choose the mediator, unlike a trial, where judges are randomly selected, sometimes not even known until the day of the trial. Not all couples are the same, and not all mediators are the same. Some are better than others. A lawyer needs to invest great consideration into finding the right match for his or her client.

Someone with a fair amount of experience generally is a mediator who can entertain a wide spectrum of solutions and is willing to think out of the box. Most importantly, a good mediator will strike the perfect balance between nurturing and efficient. He or she will bring a positive, upbeat attitude and will listen to the parties with empathy but will not allow them to go on endlessly about the past.

There is the option to attend mediation without lawyers present. I strongly recommend against this course. It turns mediation into an inefficient process since the parties will have to take every proposal back to the lawyers.

This can go on for months until an agreement is reached. The mediation process often only takes one or two days. Additionally, since the lawyers are not present to hear how a proposed resolution developed, they may, unintentionally, give unhelpful advice that puts doubts in the clients' minds. When the clients go back to mediation, all momentum is lost, and the spouses find themselves back at square one.

Many times, in mediation, a lawyer is moving towards the agreement along with the client. Being in the room, he or she witnesses the growth in the client's mindset and feels the emotional climate. The lawyer can follow the logic of a client becoming flexible regarding positions that were at one time sacred. They can perceive how the client and the spouse across the table are moving towards a 'yes'. Therefore anyone who has influence on the outcome should be in the room for these mediations. Clients think they are saving money by not having lawyers present, when they end up spending a great deal more.

Having lawyers present also increases the odds that the clients will go home with a signed agreement. At the end of the mediation, the mediator drafts a minute of settlement, which contains the general points of the agreement. The parties, including the lawyers, will sign the document before leaving the room, which will give them an enforceable deal. When an agreement isn't signed, there is the risk that one of the spouses will go home and become angry and want to revisit the issues.

This doesn't mean a lawyer or client should automatically lock into a deal. If a client expresses reservations, the lawyer should give him or her time to think it over. The lawyers can insert language into the minutes of settlement that says the agreement will take effect in 72 hours unless the mediator is contacted.

In family law, there is a tremendous amount of seller's remorse. Family lawyers are reported to the law society more often than any other type of lawyer. The complaints are almost all filed after agreements are reached. Usually, it's a case of the client still hurting, and since he or she cannot blame the spouse anymore, the lawyer becomes a convenient target. Therefore it's important for everyone to feel good about an agreement before it's signed.

ARBITRATION

Arbitration is like mediation in that a neutral, third party is brought in to facilitate an agreement. There are, however, considerable differences. Most significantly, an arbitrator can impose a binding decision, which makes him or her almost like a judge. What sets it apart from a court trial is that the parties decide how the arbitration will unfold, the rules for introducing evidence, and the issues that will be covered. The couple feels in control of the process, which will help move them away from a victim mentality.

Both mediation and arbitration are private processes. Everything can be made public in the family law court.

Privacy is a major advantage of meditation and arbitration. Once a case is brought to a courtroom, everything is made public including the spouses' misdeeds, which could prove embarrassing for them and their children. Also, meditation and arbitration save time and, therefore, money.

Through mediation and arbitration, a situation can be resolved within six months. A trial can take anywhere from twelve months to two years to complete. This emotionally exhausts you and stalls you from making any forward progress. Mediation and arbitration can also help spouses stay out of the courtroom in the future. Some final agreements may contain clauses demanding the parties first utilize mediation or arbitration in the event of a future disagreement.

Another process proving popular and effective is a hybrid of mediation and arbitration. In this alternative, the couple resolves as much as possible through mediation. When the remaining issues become too difficult to resolve, the mediator switches his hats. He becomes an arbitrator and decides the outstanding issues on his own. Like with a standard arbitration, the parties sign an agreement confirming the process as binding before the process starts.

AVOID TRIALS AT ALL COSTS

If a client insists on taking the divorce to trial, he or she needs to understand all that it might cost between $10,000–800,000. On average, it will cost ten times as much as a lawyer-assisted mediation. This is because of the amount of work done leading up to the hearing. The process in every jurisdiction is slightly different.

In all jurisdictions, a lot must happen before the trial begins. Each step takes time and money. An immense amount of hard legal work goes into preparing for a trial. There are interim court applications to file, trial conferences, preparation of evidence, etc. In a standard divorce trial, the parties first prepare a statement of claim which is served to the other side. Then the other party has an opportunity to respond to the claim.

During this time, lawyers are busy preparing any documents they will share with the other side and enter into the court proceedings— recordings of assets, medical records, proof of infidelity, etc. Meanwhile, the lawyers on both sides may be billing hundreds of hours. Then, in the period leading up to the trial, depositions are taken. Over the course of a day or two, the spouses are questioned, under oath, in front of a court reporter. The transcripts are entered into the court record to be used at the trial.

Preparing for a trial is like putting on a play. If the clients have money, then it will open on Broadway. The lawyers will have prepared the clients' testimony, often running them through mock cross-examinations. They will also have planned lines of attack for when they question the other spouse and supporting witnesses.

An opening statement will have been carefully crafted and looked over by several of the team's lawyers. They'll have taken time to state a case for introducing certain evidence, and planned arguments to dismiss evidence brought by the opposing side. Crafting closing arguments is another time-consuming task.

At a typical Broadway-style trial, a minimum of two lawyers will attend the trial, and lawyers aren't known for offering two for the price of one. This is the effort it takes to pull off a quality trial. If one client has less money, then he or she will have to settle for an off-off-Broadway production. Thoroughness is sacrificed, meaning the client has less of a shot at obtaining his or her desired outcome. Most of the cases will settle before trial, some even on the courtroom steps, but well after most of the work has been finished and the money has been spent.

If a trial is brought to completion, the judge will take anywhere from thirty days to six months to issue a ruling. In rare instances, it takes judges an entire year. During this time, clients will be suffering in a state of limbo. They will be waiting for a decision before deciding the next step in their lives. How can someone decide where to live or work if he or she doesn't know how much money there will be?

The divorce may not even necessarily end with the ruling. Both sides can appeal the decision, a process that can last another year and cost tens of thousands of dollars more. Unless you're a multimillionaire, the trial process has the potential to bankrupt you. Believe it or not, there are clients who will live with this outcome because it's preferable to letting go.

If you're forced to go through a trial, the most important thing is to act as authentically as possible. Judges can tell when someone is trying to pull the wool over their eyes. Obviously, one is legally required to tell the truth, but some people try to twist stories and situations to gain sympathy.

This is a guaranteed way to quickly lose the court's respect and, ultimately, can have major ramifications on the judge's decision. Don't be afraid to take responsibility for the situation instead of spending your time in court pointing an accusatory finger at your spouse. When someone plays the role of a victim, people eventually see him or her as anything but that.

In the end, when a couple decides to go to trial, they are electing to place their future in the hands of a broken system. Law is a heavily regulated, rule-oriented business that is slow to change. Precedent rules, which means decisions are being made based on cases from the past. The law is not concerned with the present reality or hopes for a different future. Looking backward when trying to move forward damages progress.

In Canada, the law is steeped in tradition. Judges are called 'lords' and 'ladies', co-counsel is referred to as 'learned friend'. Such formality promotes civility, but it also fosters stodginess and in-the-box thinking. Tradition is useful for providing inspiration but doing something simply because this is the way it has always been done is not a compelling reason, especially when we stop questioning whether the tradition is to our benefit. Lawyers tend to have a lofty sense of themselves.

After all, they are smart and well-educated people in a highly reputable business. Because of this, they are overly concerned with reputation, which makes them risk-averse. A lawyer with such concerns will follow precedent and not go out on a limb to come up with unorthodox solutions. The Richard Bransons of the world are not practicing law.

A family dispute is not the same as an intellectual property argument. Every family is different and unique. If rules and regulations take center stage, it becomes impossible to hear what the litigants are saying would be the right answer for this family. Culturally, certain answers may pose problems for certain families, or a specific type of arrangement is needed to fit an exceptional set of needs.

TIMES ARE CHANGING

In family law, lawyers and courts should be looking for more creative, innovative ways of resolving disputes that are more affordable and take a fraction of the time. Fortunately, lawyers don't have a monopoly on the conflict resolution business.

A multitude of helping professionals, like counselors, mediators, and arbitrators, can help couples solve disputes.

Once people become aware of other effective options for conflict resolution, lawyers will price themselves out of a job if all they can offer clients are costly, prolonged trials.

People are slowly waking up to these other possibilities. When I started practicing law in British Columbia, Canada, over twenty-five years ago, 10% of family law litigants were self-represented. Today, the number is around 70% in Toronto, Canada.

This is not ideal. Thinking they can go to trial without paying anything more than court costs, couples don't think twice about bringing litigation to court over the most minor issues, and judges end up playing the role of lawyers, and the court gets overwhelmed by cases. Hopefully, couples will soon become more familiar with lower-cost, time-efficient alternatives like face-to-face negotiations, mediation, and arbitration.

Ideally, forward-thinking legislation would remove family disputes out of the courtroom and automatically place them in a mediation or arbitration type process. This would prove efficient and respect the couple's privacy. In a trial, the judge has a sense of how he or she will rule by noon of the first day. Everyone is forced to sit through another seven days of arguments, evidence, and testimony, so there is a feeling of justice.

There is not a great amount of political determination to shift family law cases from the courtroom to mediation and arbitration. It's not a trendy topic like immigration or war, even if it affects almost everyone. A divorcee filing for bankruptcy will impact the lives of his or her family members, friends and colleagues.

Even if the couple has money, a trial is a major distraction, both emotionally and physically. You're putting all your dirty laundry on display for your community, family and children to see. You can look at court judgments online for $6. I just filled a lawsuit against my old law firm, Hart Legal, and other lawyers messaged me right away asking about it.

Maybe you're the rare person who has nothing to hide, but do you want people, especially your children, to see you engaged in such nastiness? Don't you want them to see you use the next two years of your life in a productive, positive fashion?

Most importantly, they need to see that life's obstacles won't stop you in your tracks. This, after all, is how you want them to approach all of life's inevitable challenges. It is important for you as a parent to make the transition as painless for your child as possible. The alternative is choosing to fight. You should know that several years down the road, as you reflect on this moment in your life, you will look at it with profound sadness and deep disappointment.

CHAPTER 7

STARTING YOUR NEW LIFE OFF RIGHT

"Kate"

Kate, barely twenty years old, was an attractive woman leading a somewhat boring existence when she met Jack, a handsome man in his mid-thirties. She came from a single-mother household, and Jack offered her stability. She was also attracted to his fondness for partying and having fun. This allowed her to live the life of a young person while still maintaining a degree of emotional and physical security. Soon, Jack introduced Kate to the party lifestyle. Although unenthusiastic about this interest, she went along with it.

For the most part, they were happy and a suitable match. Together, they started a home furnishing store. The business expanded and became quite profitable. Eventually, they could afford to buy a house that sat on an impressive piece of land. In a matter of less than ten years, Kate had matured from a young woman into a person with professional and domestic responsibilities. Now thirty, her outlook on marriage had started to evolve, as well. No longer did she accept her husband being physically involved with other women. She felt the lifestyle damaged the relationship. She also thought it was time to consider starting a family.

Jack didn't share his wife's desire for a traditional marriage. He was completely dismissive of her wishes and carried on as if nothing had changed. After seeing that he made no attempt to even appreciate her mindset, she decided divorce was the only option. Here, too, he adopted an indifferent approach, indicating that he would take no active role in moving the divorce forward. In fact, he made it impossible for her to access their personal and business bank accounts, daring her to retain a lawyer to attain entry. These tactics were designed to control Kate and keep her in the marriage.

She came into ClearWay Law for a meeting, and our lawyers didn't have encouraging news for her. Because of how her husband set up the business and registered the titles to the property, it would take time to negotiate a divorce. Our lawyers laid out the cost in terms of time, money, and emotions. It would require a lot of money since it seemed as if her husband was far from adopting the growth mindset that would allow him to negotiate generously.

That night, she reflected on our conversation. She was young and didn't want to waste her prime fighting her husband. Having already built a life from scratch once before, there was no reason she could not do it again. She loaded up her car the next morning with whatever clothes and personal possessions would fit and drove one thousand miles to start life in a different city.

This meant leaving everything behind including her stake in the business and the property shared with her husband. Not having children made leaving easier but walking away from what was her life— and a substantial amount of money— took incredible inner strength and was certainly helped by her willingness to take ownership of the situation. She took a wholly spiritual approach to the matter.

She said to me, "It's just stuff I'm leaving behind. I have many years ahead of me to acquire new stuff." Instead of allowing any money she was forgoing to cause insecurity, she felt secure from the little money in her possession, and she freed herself from an unhealthy marriage earlier than most people manage, giving her a head start on her new life.

Ten years after letting go, Kate has rebuilt her life. She works as an administrator at a hospital while pursuing a lifelong interest in acting. For seven years she has been married to a man she calls her soul mate, and they have two children together. Most importantly, she doesn't regret her decision to leave and believes it was worth every penny relinquished. This new life was made possible by her determination to not allow her past relationship to bog her down.

From the moment she sped away from her life with Jack, she didn't spend a second thinking about him and the real injustices thrown her way. She lived in the present and thought about where the road was going to take her. Not everyone can adopt this mentality. Some people, especially those with children, need to negotiate the right financial settlement. They can't afford to pay for children alone.

Kate's story reminds me of the opening scene from the movie *Easy Rider*. After concluding a major drug transaction, Wyatt and Billy hop on their motorcycles to make the trip from Los Angeles to New Orleans so that they can attend Mardi Gras. Before they tear down the highway, Wyatt removes his watch and tosses it into the dirt, as if to show his desire for freedom and unwillingness to be constrained by other people's conventions.

What's amazing is that Kate came to this understanding at such a young age. Usually, it's not until people reach the age of forty-five, when half of life is in the rear-view mirror, that they begin to ask questions about the meaning of life, the quality of their relationships, and the value of material possessions. A person starts realizing that much of what they've acquired in terms of possessions doesn't come with them when they die.

These musings should prompt the realization that to be truly free means living a life not defined by other people's desires or expectations. This doesn't imply living a selfish life. Rather, it's about feeling as if the person has full control of his or her choices. A nurse in England writes that, from what she has witnessed, the most common regret people express at the end of their lives is: "I wish I'd had the courage to live a life true to myself, not the life others expected of me."7

A HEALTHY MARRIAGE IS ABOUT FREEDOM

True freedom is a state of mind where one feels they can lead a life of one's choosing. If divorce can provide you with anything, it's a moment to evaluate your life, so you can begin moving in the direction of feeling free. Marriage often prevents people from taking this move towards freedom. To many people, marriage can feel tiring. They stay married for many years because they are afraid of how others will view them if they divorce, or they don't want to hurt their spouse's feelings.

Even though marriage brings two people together, it doesn't mean the parties become responsible for each other's happiness. Spouses should provide each other with enough support, so each can lead emotionally free lives. If you know who you are and where you're headed, and this is causing conflict with your spouse, to a degree where you find yourself holding back from your desires, then you need to think about moving on.

Bob

Years ago, Bob had, what he considered at the time, a serious girlfriend. They had been together for several years when Bob told her that a friend and him were taking a six-month trip through Australia and New Zealand to mark the completion of their university studies. Her anger and disappointment in Bob was intense. Bob knew he had deep feelings for her, but he was in his early twenties, and it was probably the last opportunity to take a world-traveling adventure like this before starting a career and family.

The goodbye was emotional, and during the trip, despite numerous opportunities to connect with other women, Bob stayed devoted to the girlfriend back home. Even though it was before email and cell phones, he managed to write or call almost every day for six months. In Thailand, Bob bought her a friendship ring with a ruby gemstone, which he carried in his pocket for the final three months of the trip.

It was when Bob stopped in Los Angeles on the way home to visit a friend that he called the girlfriend and sensed something had changed. Suddenly, she was telling Bob not to hurry home. When he returned the next week, they went down to the beach, and he presented her with the ruby ring, at which point, she told him that she had cheated on him with another man while he was away and was breaking up with Bob.

What Bob remembered about that moment, more than anything, was the emotion he felt. Not anger, or bitterness, but relief. Here she was freeing him of this burden he had carried on his shoulders across the other side of the world for the last six months. It felt like the heavens were opening and sunshine was pouring down. At that point, Bob realized that their relationship had been based, not on love, but obligation and duty.

It was a lesson learned that one should not stick with a relationship unless there is unconditional love between both parties. The point of the story is that Bob had enough self-awareness at such a young age to push forward with his plans for the trip. Most people are not so fortunate. Countless others, stuck in relationships allow a sense of duty and obligation to stop them from going on trips, taking spiritual journeys, and pursuing certain interests. In short, they prevent themselves from leading the lives they want to lead.

You will never achieve great things or find emotional peace unless you're leading the life you want. How long will you stay motivated if you're doing something simply to meet another person's expectations? Eventually, you will resent the person for putting you in that position from preventing you from pursuing your passion.

> *"You learn more about somebody at the end of a relationship than at the beginning."*
> —*Karen Salmansohn*

Often the grass isn't greener on the other side. If children are involved, you and your partner owe it to them to try keeping the family intact. If your spouse is not encouraging you to be the best person you can and want to be, then you must move on. Being with the right person, someone whose only demand is that you follow your heart is inspirational. The person becomes your rock, and you feel as if you can tackle the world, every boulder placed in your path appearing as nothing larger than a pebble.

Telling your spouse you want a divorce, or mutually deciding as a couple to end the marriage, is the highest hurdle to get over. Once you get past this painful moment, you need to see it as the jumping off point to a much better place. If you're on the receiving end of such news, you should ask yourself why you would stay in love with this person who is not in love with you? What would it say about your sense of self-worth? The pain of rejection is understandable, and the fear of change is to be expected, but neither are good enough reasons to spend your days pining for the past.

TODAY IS WHEN YOUR CHANGE YOUR LIFE

Sometimes a changed mindset is just a matter of changing certain elements and routines in your life. Clearing away the debris provides you with a better view of yourself and the life in front of you. The actor Denzel Washington once said about his struggles with alcohol, "I made a commitment to cut out drinking and anything that might hamper me from getting my mind and body together. And the floodgates of goodness have opened upon me— spiritually and financially." He was stuck in the bottle, but once he chose to flip that switch and free himself, it was as seamless as moving from night to day.

Merely coming to the realization that a marriage is preventing you from actualizing your best self is not enough. You cannot articulate the ways it's working against you. Further, you need to pin down how you found yourself involved in this less than ideal situation. Without this understanding, you will soon find yourself in a new relationship full of the same old problems and patterns.

Freedom becomes a possibility when you begin breaking old patterns and approaching life from a completely different angle. As Albert Einstein said, "Insanity is doing the same thing over and over again and expecting different results."

The misery of a disappointing marriage doesn't become easier to absorb the second or third time around. If anything, it becomes sharper because accompanying any pain is the frustration of helplessness.

"Phil"

Phil is the perfect example of someone who is constantly repeating past mistakes. He came to me when his first marriage was unraveling. He had met his wife through a service that connected men with women from the Ukraine. They knew each other for only several weeks before they married. The marriage lasted less than four years. They had two children during this time.

The divorce was costly, especially for a man who makes a moderate salary as a police officer. Two years later he married a second Ukrainian woman, also introduced to him through the agency. He explained his fondness for these women as a deep attraction to the type, a fetish of sorts. This marriage lasted only three years and produced one child. This meant more spousal and child support.

After the second divorce, he acknowledged not having learned his lesson from the first marriage. He didn't seem to have learned his lesson. Any diagnosis was superficial at best, like thinking the problem lay in his not having taken more time to get to know these women.

Meanwhile, he was ignoring this emerging pattern of traveling halfway across the world to find a wife. In my opinion, his problem was obvious. He married these women from the Ukraine because he didn't want an equal partnership. These are women who tend to be submissive. They are arriving from a foreign country and are agreeing to this non-traditional arrangement because they, and their families back home, desperately need the money.

They don't want to risk the cash cow, so they obey. Obviously, this is a poor foundation for a marriage. What happens is that, over time, the women feel more comfortable in their adopted country, especially after they have children. They learn the language and adopt the culture, which includes appreciating how women are to behave and treated in society. Like any person with self-respect, they begin demanding an equal role in the relationship. They voice their opinions.

Phil, not abandoning hope he could find a young woman interested in playing the role of a submissive wife, remarried for a third time to another Ukrainian woman. He's now separated from this woman. Hopefully, this divorce will open his eyes to his sexist attitudes towards women. It is costing him his retirement, relationships with his children, and a productive and happy life.

Unfortunately, there is no real indication he is about to change. In a recent phone call, he said that these women show no appreciation for him having showed them better lives. He sees himself as the victim. Until he becomes more self-reflective and switches his mindset, he will continue this limited existence.

In the movie *Groundhog Day*, Bill Murray plays an arrogant weatherman who finds himself stuck in a time loop, forced to repeat the same day again and again. At first, he uses his situation to womanize, drink, and steal, but he continuously fails to gain the one thing he wants most of all, the heart and affection of Rita. He decides to change course and begins using his knowledge of how the day will unfold to help the people of the town.

The rest of his time is spent becoming a renaissance man. Eventually, this new authentic self impresses Rita, and he is finally able to break free from the time loop. This is a movie about a person becoming more aware of his impact on other people and his environment and then deciding to break the cycle and gain his freedom, by simply changing his routine and approach.

Do you want to live the same day over again? If you're happy, then this is not a bad world to wake up to. If you're miserable, it becomes easy to start believing that this is all your life has to offer, that these are the only types of relationships available to you. If now is not the right time to break the pattern, when will it be?

When the children are out of high school? When they are out of college? After they are married? How many years can you stand to wait? The time to take advantage of your life is now. You only get one go-around.

Think how fortunate you're to be alive. One egg and one sperm combined to create you, and you live in a world of abundance, one full of opportunities, and it's your obligation to take advantage of these offerings.

The belief that future events will turn out for the best is the cornerstone of all positive divorces. Divorce will force you to look in the mirror, reflect on your life and come to a better understanding of your self, but if this introspection is not layered with the hope that something grander will be gained from this moment, then it will quickly devolve into sadness for all that was lost.

CONNECT TO YOURSELF

I have been told that my talent lies at shortening the distance between people. This is true. When I attend parties, I busy myself with connecting people and making sure the conversation is free-flowing. Witnessing rich conversations between people makes me genuinely happy.

This is a useful talent that I encourage our lawyers to use in negotiating a divorce. It can help the parties get a better understanding of each other's perspectives and develop ways to complement the perspectives without causing a sense of alienation on either side. It's an interest-based negotiation approach. As the years have gone by, however, I've begun to realize that the greatest and most beneficial challenge is not shortening the distance between spouses but shortening the distance a client has within him or herself.

John Wooden is hailed as the greatest college basketball coach of all time. He in no way was the average coach who motivated his players by cursing at them, throwing chairs or yelling at them for losing. Someone who acts this way is not a true coach since this is not how one provides guidance for a way forward. All it does is ask the players to make amends for the past as if they hurt the coach.

Coach Wooden was a growth-minded individual who never saw losing or failure as the issue. For him, the primary focus was on being the best person possible and knowing everything else would fall into place.

> *"Success is never final. Failure is never fatal.*
>
> *It's courage that counts."*
>
> —*Coach Wooden*

Most people can never arrive at a better place because they act as their own judge. They are too quick to assess each victory or setback as an end rather than another step-in life's long journey.

Ultimately, divorce isn't about the other person; it's about you and the choices you made. The real journey, therefore, is working to understand, appreciate and love yourself. When you arrive at this point of acceptance, you're relieved of the burden of depending on someone else to provide you with peace, joy, and satisfaction.

Once, you become self-aware and can recognize the thinking patterns and processes in your head, you will begin forcing out of your life the people who contribute negatively to your thinking, like how a recovering drug addict is told to stay away from his or her old friends. A growth-minded person is constantly changing his or her circle of acquaintances. If a forty-five-year-old man is still hanging out exclusively with his college buddies, this a clear sign that no real growth is happening in his life.

It's normal and healthy to grow out of relationships and move in a different direction. Society makes us feel as if we are acting disloyal when we abandon relationships but cultivating new friendships and business acquaintances and opportunities is a thrilling sensation. Sometimes even a new plutonic relationship can feel like a schoolyard crush. This is a feeling of rejuvenation. You're tapping into an unexplored side of your self. This taste is a preview of the life of possibilities and opportunities available to you in the next stage of your life once you break free.

> *"Things turn out best for the people who make*
> *the best of the way things turn out,"*
> —*Coach Wooden*

"Scott"

At twenty-one, right after walking down at his college graduation, Scott took a stroll down the marriage aisle with his college-sweetheart, Stephanie, the only woman he ever seriously dated. The couple had three children before they turned thirty. During this time, Scott's life changed substantially. He discovered a passion for finance, went back to school to complete an advanced degree and, within a couple of years, had become a success in the wealth management world. His wife was not pleased with the changes in Scott's life.

At the outset of the marriage, she had envisioned a different style of domestic life than Scott was willing or able to deliver. The tension became unbearable for Scott. He found his eyes wandering, and he began flirting with other women, although he would never take it to an inappropriate level. Instead, the frustration and unhappiness he felt in his marriage gathered, and he realized he would never feel content living the life his wife wanted him to lead. Further, he could not feel satisfied with accomplishing any business goals because it came with a guilty sense he was letting his family down.

Scott took responsibility for the marriage's demise, but he also understood that his shifting values and interests didn't make him a bad person. He appreciated that some of life's poor choices are made because people lack the life experience needed to make better choices.

He carried out the settlement negotiations in a spirit of generosity. He provided Stephanie with considerable resources for her and the children. A couple of years after finalizing the divorce, Scott married a woman he refers to as his 'soul mate'. She works in finance, as well, and is deeply supportive of Scott's financial ambitions. They are true partners in all aspects of life. His eyes are no longer wandering for something better. In business, he is more successful than ever, as if the new wife has inspired him to reach great heights.

His spirit of generosity, no question, played a major role in actualizing this great new life. The openness he showed towards taking responsibility for his faults, his gratefulness for Stephanie's fine parenting, and his appreciativeness of the importance of carrying out an amicable divorce indicated a general receptiveness to the possibilities the world had to offer.

Conclusion

In Napoleon Hill's 1937 self-improvement business book, *Think and Grow Rich*, a twenty-five-year study of the most successful people on the planet, the author lists thirty major causes for why people fail in life to reach their goals. On the list is 'Wrong selection of a mate in marriage'. The trouble is that people have difficulty treating this misstep as a mistake, one that is better to live with than to correct. According to this outlook, the correction, divorce, is incorrectly seen as a failure of epic proportions. The road towards a better future begins with accepting the idea that taking responsibility for a problematic marriage doesn't make someone a bad person.

You, too, deserve a smooth divorce. You have the power to let go of your former spouse and relationship and learn from the past to avoid repeating the same mistakes in the future. If none of this were possible, there would be no reason for this book. But you must make the decision to change your mindset today.

I dare you to not let a past relationship define your existence. Your reason for waking up in the morning should not be so you can go to your lawyer's office to stick the screws in your spouse or punish him or her by keeping the children away.

Put yourself in an emotional and mental place where you can respond, and not react, to a challenge. Responding means taking a deep breath and thinking about how your reaction will resolve the challenge in a beneficial manner, as opposed to generating more drama and hate.

If you're overly sensitive to every unkind word and action thrown your way, then make an effort to deal with your sensitivities. If you have a temper, don't simply accept it as a feature of your personality. You can do work, through therapy or other means, to get your anger under control. Reactive behavior works within the framework of the past. A responsive person, on the other hand, is a creator. He or she looks for a different path forward.

This type of mindset will spill into all other areas of life, whether it's a new way of engaging the children, conducting business, or interacting with friends. When someone is creating, they are discovering more efficient, innovative, and profound ways of living. By finding new ways to engage, you're adding value to what already exists, as opposed to sticking to a routine that further degrades what at one time you cherished. You will begin to feel as if anything is possible.

I dare you to find your purpose in life. Many marriages fail because one spouse sees the other as his or her reason for living. He or she feels as if life without the person fails to have meaning. Such dependency is not reasonable or healthy. It becomes a responsibility, a terrible weight, for both people in the relationship to carry. The purpose you find in life is what should make you happy, and the relationship is there to provide a steady foundation, so you have the confidence to pursue your passion without fear of failing.

The time to act is now. If you know your relationship is not right and unsalvageable, then why are you committed to staying? Is it fear of the unknown? Are you afraid of how family and friends will react? Do you not want to hurt your spouse's feelings? Are you hesitant to create an unstable situation for your children? Is having less money a concern? These are all fear-based reasons.

This should be an indication that you're in the wrong relationship. Put those reasons on the shelf and then ask whether you should end the marriage? If the answer is yes, then consider how and why you're allowing all these external factors to prevent you from acting on your own desires and needs. If you stay, you will only build resentment towards your spouse, children, and family for making you feel as if you had no choice. But you do have the choice to shift your thinking and take control of your life and not live it for other people. All those fears are nothing but challenges that will be resolved with the right frame of mind and the right people helping you, so you can move forward with compassion and a sense of empowerment and become a creator producing a wondrous future.

About ClearWay Law

ClearWay Law is a law firm in Toronto Canada that is opening offices throughout Canada, and one day in India, England, and China. Through our referral network with other lawyers across Canada, we can manage any of your legal issues. We can find you a lawyer for the following areas of law:

- Real estate law
- Immigration to Canada and the USA
- Business law
- Family Law

- ⅄ Getting Married or Divorced
- ⅄ Marriage agreement
- ⅄ Estate Disputes
- ⅄ Personal injury (car accidents)

We offer Chinese service. Send us an email in Chinese to jxu@clearwaylaw.com

ClearWay Law plans to open consulting offices in Beijing in 2019. You can contact us 24/7.

ENDNOTES

1 Feldstein Family Law Group, "Divorce Fact Sheet 2016," http://canadianbudgetbinder.com/wp-content/uploads/2016/10/FELDSTEIN-FAMILY-LAW-Divorce-Fact-Sheet-2016.pdf.

2 Roger Friedman, "Jane Fonda Dishes on Ted Turner in Book," April 5, 2005, Foxnews.com http://www.foxnews.com/story/2005/04/05/jane-fonda-dishes-on-ted-turner-in-book.html.

3 Sara Reistad-Long, "Dr. Oz's Tips for a Happy Marriage," April 4, 2012, http://www.womansday.com/relationships/dating-marriage/advice/a6469/dr-oz-marriage-tips.

4 Lina Das, "'High on Drugs, Steve McQueen Jammed the Gun Against My Head,'" May 2, 2015, http://www.dailymail.co.uk/home/event/article-3062535/Steve-McQueen-wife-Neile-Adams.html.

5 Carol S. Dweck, *Mindset: The New Psychology of Success* (New York: Ballantine Books, 2016).

6 Harry Benson, "Divorce has a devastating impact on children. But two factors make the big difference," November 24, 2014, https://marriagefoundationblog.wordpress.com/2014/11/24/divorce-has-a-devastating-impact-on-children-how-many-more-studies-do-we-need.

7   Sarah Ridley, "Dying People's Top Five Regrets Revealed and They May Just Change Your Life," March 17, 2015, http://www.mirror.co.uk/news/world-news/dying-peoples-top-5-regrets-5348209.

*Clients in this story are not real clients of ClearWay Law.

CPSIA information can be obtained
at www.ICGtesting.com
Printed in the USA
BVHW030208030620
580833BV00001B/163